PARENTS' EMERGENCY INF[...]

D0360739

Doctor's Name _____

Address _____

Phone Numbers _____ _____
                    daytime   after hours

Dentist's Name _____

Phone Number _____

Children's Birthdates _____ _____
                           name   birthday

_____ _____
        name   birthday

_____ _____
        name   birthday

_____ _____
        name   birthday

Fire Department/Rescue Squad _____

Police _____ Ambulance _____

Poison Control Center _____ Dog Warden _____

Hospital _____ _____
              name   address

Best Route to Hospital _____

_____

Drugstore/Pharmacy _____

Parents' Phone Numbers _____ _____
                            mother's home   mother's work

_____ _____
     father's home   father's work

Closest Neighbor/Relative _____
                               name

_____ _____
     phone   address

1

The Parents' Guide to
Baby & Child
Medical Care

by the Meadowbrook Medical Reference Group
edited by Terril H. Hart, M.D.

Meadowbrook Press
18318 Minnetonka Boulevard
Deephaven, MN 55391

Second printing March 1983

Printed in the United States of America

Library of Congress CIP Data

The Parents' guide to baby and child medical care.

    Bibliography: p.
    Includes index.
    1. Pediatrics—Popular works. 2. Children—Care and hygiene. 3. Infants—Care and hygiene. I. Hart, Terril H., 1939-   . II. Meadowbrook Medical Reference Group.
RJ61.P2245   1982   618.92   82-14120
ISBN 0-915658-58-5
ISBN 0-915658-57-7 (pbk.)

ISBN (paperback) 0-915658-57-7
ISBN (hardcover) 0-915658-58-5

Medical Editor: Terril H. Hart, M.D.
Editor: Kathe Grooms
Designer: Terry Dugan
Design Assistant: Sandra Falls
Production Manager: John Ware
Illustrator: Doug Oudekerk
Writer/Researchers: Steve Grooms, Kathy Hanson

Special thanks to Brian Baysinger, Jan Brust, Ruth Chalk, Martha Fisk, Neal Kielar, Sue Kirchoff, Julie Smith, and Julie Yoder for their invaluable help in the preparation of this book.
    The contents of this book have been reviewed and checked for accuracy and appropriateness of application by medical doctors. However, the authors, editors, reviewers and publisher disclaim all responsibility arising from any adverse effects or results which occur or might occur as a result of the inappropriate application of any of the information contained in this book. If you have any question or concern about the appropriateness or application of the treatments described in this book, consult your health care professional.

Medical Consultants

Table of Contents

8

PART IV: APPENDIX

CHARTS AND TABLES

Introduction

As a pediatrician, I know how important good, solid information is for a child's health. If you're a well-informed parent, you respond more effectively to your child's illnesses and injuries. You feel self-assured and confident, whether you're treating a problem yourself or contacting professional help. Your child thus receives better health care overall, simply because problems are caught early and treated correctly.

I've also discovered that the medical information that parents need has never been available in a form that is fast and easy to use. The venerable Dr. Spock's advice is set forth in paragraph form, making it necessary for a worried parent to isolate the crucial treatment information from background and explanation. Other books present elaborate diagrams or stark cartoons in attempts to make essential information more readable, but parents tell me that those formats don't work out appreciably better than the paragraph treatment. Finally, these books are most widely available as perfect bound paperbacks, which oblige parents to hold them open while using them and which then fall apart after only limited use.

This book is designed to solve those problems. Panels of health professionals and parents have exhaustively reviewed its contents and design. Its guidelines are based on the knowledge and experience of many health care professionals. In contrast to some of the old standard references, it also includes the most recent thinking and treatment plans in pediatrics.

Moreover, it has been designed to make information as fast to get at as possible. You can tell at a glance whether your child's illness or injury is one you can treat yourself or one that requires professional advice or care. For problems you can treat at home, supplies and treatment are clearly laid out in numbered steps or bulleted items, and they are illustrated whenever necessary. The spiral binding allows you to lay the book open—which is essential for the life-saving emergency procedures—and also insures years of use without a broken binding or lost pages.

I think you'll agree that this book makes it easier for you to meet the responsibility of giving your child the best health care available. I wish good health to you both!

Terril H. Hart, M.D.
Wayzata, MN

Part 1

Keeping Your Child Healthy

There's nothing as pleasing as the sight of a healthy, happy child going about her business, unaware of your attention. Making sure your child is well cared for, both on a day-to-day basis and in the long run, will give her the best chance of continuing a happy, carefree existence throughout her childhood. Good health now will be a sound foundation for many years to come.

Preventive Care

Most parents these days are well aware that a simple program of preventive care will both lessen the chances of their children getting sick and reduce the cost of the care needed to help them get well. Regular visits for shots and checkups—when your child is healthy—will diminish the number of "irregular" visits she'll need because she's sick. And if your doctor sees your child on a regular basis, she will be better able to pick up on any unusual patterns of growth or development and thus catch problems early.

There are other benefits to following a good preventive health plan for your child. If she's used to seeing the doctor for regular well-child checkups, she won't be as likely to associate health care with pain and discomfort and therefore may be less frightened when an illness arises. And finally, as your child grows up, the pattern of taking charge of health through preventive care and good health habits will contribute to her continued well-being.

RECOMMENDED CHECKUP SCHEDULE

The guidelines below can help you plan a preventive health care program for your child. They represent the thinking of the Committee on Practice and Ambulatory Medicine in the American

	INFANCY						EARLY CHILDHOOD				
	By 1 mo.	2 mos.	4 mos.	6 mos.	9 mos.	12 mos.	15 mos.	18 mos.	24 mos.	3 yrs.	4 yrs.
PHYSICAL EXAMINATION	●	●	●	●	●	●	●	●	●	●	●
MEDICAL HISTORY (Health Profile)	●	●	●	●	●	●	●	●	●	●	●
MEASUREMENTS Height/Weight	●	●	●	●	●	●	●	●	●	●	●
Head Circumference	●	●	●	●	●	●					
TESTS/ SCREENINGS Vision	●	●	●	●	●	●	●	●	●	●	●
Hearing	●	●	●	●	●	●	●	●	●	●	●
Blood Pressure										●	●
Blood Tests*					●				●		
Urinalysis*				●					●		
Heredity/Metabolic	●										
DENTAL CHECKUP**										●	
DEVELOPMENT/ BEHAVIOR ASSESSMENT	●	●	●	●	●	●	●	●	●	●	●
GENERAL CONSULTATION (as needed)	●	●	●	●	●	●	●	●	●	●	●

*At least once during infancy, early childhood, late childhood and adolescence.
**Initial visit at 2½-3 years and every 6 months thereafter.

RECOMMENDED CHECKUP SCHEDULE

Academy of Pediatrics. Naturally, if your child develops health problems that need further attention, you will see health care professionals more frequently, but preventive care should minimize that need.

	LATE CHILDHOOD					ADOLESCENCE			
	5 yrs.	6 yrs.	8 yrs.	10 yrs.	12 yrs.	14 yrs.	16 yrs.	18 yrs.	20 yrs.
PHYSICAL EXAMINATION	●	●	●	●	●	●	●	●	●
MEDICAL HISTORY (Health Profile)	●	●	●	●	●	●	●	●	●
MEASUREMENTS Height/Weight Head Circumference	●	●	●	●	●	●	●	●	●
TESTS/ SCREENINGS									
Vision	●	●	●	●	●	●	●	●	●
Hearing	●	●	●	●	●	●	●	●	●
Blood Pressure	●	●	●	●	●	●	●	●	●
Blood Tests*			●					●	
Urinalysis*			●					●	
Heredity/Metabolic									
DENTAL CHECKUP**									
DEVELOPMENT/ BEHAVIOR ASSESSMENT	●	●	●	●	●	●	●	●	●
GENERAL CONSULTATION (as needed)	●	●	●	●	●	●	●	●	●

*At least once during infancy, early childhood, late childhood and adolescence.
**Initial visit at 2½-3 years and every 6 months thereafter.

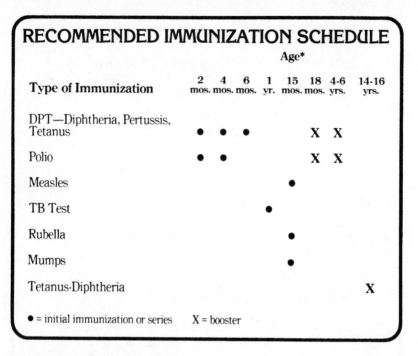

RECOMMENDED IMMUNIZATION SCHEDULE

| | Age* | | | | | | | |
Type of Immunization	2 mos.	4 mos.	6 mos.	1 yr.	15 mos.	18 mos.	4-6 yrs.	14-16 yrs.
DPT—Diphtheria, Pertussis, Tetanus	●	●	●				X	X
Polio	●	●					X	X
Measles					●			
TB Test				●				
Rubella					●			
Mumps					●			
Tetanus-Diphtheria								X

● = initial immunization or series   X = booster

Choosing a Doctor

The major choice you'll have to make in choosing a doctor for your child is between a pediatrician and a family physician. Both are fully trained specialists, but a pediatrician focuses on children's health and growth, while a family practitioner focuses on the health and growth of each member of the family. Whichever type of health care professional you prefer, we recommend that you select and meet with the doctor you have chosen before your child is born

Nurses, nurse practitioners and paramedical personnei will also play roles in your child's health care. As you choose a doctor, find out about whether these assistants are available to handle the routine care, for their contributions will increase the breadth of health care your child can receive.

The chart on pages 18-19 outlines the major questions you should ask a doctor before settling into a long-term relationship.

- Ask neighbors, relatives, school staff members and others about their arrangements for medical care. Check print sources as well—yellow pages, a doctors' directory at your local library, and so on.

- Follow up with preliminary calls to the top prospects' offices to get a sketch of each practice (see p. 25).

- Schedule an introductory visit (before your child is born, if you're expecting, and before your child is sick, if you're changing doctors).
- Use the visit to cover any of the more detailed questions you'd like to raise, see the facilities, and get acquainted.

Accident Prevention

Because of improved preventive health care and other advances in medicine, childhood diseases that formerly killed children have been largely eliminated or controlled. Today, accidents kill more children than the next five causes of death combined.

It isn't productive to overprotect children, even though ordinarily children learn from their mistakes. But children must be protected from accidents that could be fatal or disabling. Remove dangers and instruct your child in safe practices, even if you think he is too young to understand.

Most accidents happen at "odd" moments and when parents and children are under stress. When family members are ill or distressed or daily rituals are interrupted, children often are ignored. They are then much more likely to get into trouble they would otherwise avoid.

Automobiles

More children are killed in auto accidents than in any other way. Yet almost all of these deaths are preventable.

- Use an officially approved car seat or restraint that's appropriate for your child's size.
- Insist that your child is properly secured before beginning every trip, short or long, starting with your trip home from the hospital. This is the single most important measure you can take to improve your child's chances for surviving to adulthood. If you make this a standard policy, you will have no arguments.

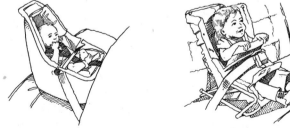

- Car seats for infants under 20 lbs. should face toward the rear of the car; carriers for children over 20 lbs. should face forward.

CHECKLIST FOR CHOOSING A DOCTOR

The following checklist should help you in identifying and narrowing down your choices of candidates for the best doctor you can find.

Basic Information

Name _____

Address _____

Phone (office) _____

       (24-hour answering service) _____

Hospital affiliation(s) _____

_____

Accepting new patients? Yes ___ No ___

Type of Professionals in Office

___ pediatrician or ___ family practitioner
___ board certified or ___ board eligible
___ pediatric nurse-practitioner
___ physician's assistant or "P.A."

Type of Practice

___ solo practice or ___ group practice

Professional Affiliations (check one or more)

___ teaching appointment at a university
___ on hospital medical staff
___ member of professional medical group(s)

Basic Services

___ sees patients by appointment only
___ allows walk-in visits
___ practice covered at all times
___ allows at least 15 minutes per routine visit
___ thorough baseline history plus current medical records kept
___ medical records open to patients concerned
___ gives advice on the phone
___ maximum 2-week wait for routine visit (except late summer)

Accessibility

___ bus or nearby public transportation
___ wheelchair accessible
___ wheelchair available
___ free parking nearby

Special Services

___ babysitting
___ patient-education classes offered or encouraged
___ patient-advocate services
___ interpreter (for languages other than English, or for hearing impaired)

Medical/Laboratory Services

___ x-ray in building or nearby
___ minor surgery in office
___ treats fractures
___ blood tests
___ cardiograms
___ casting and minor orthopedic services
___ urine tests, strep tests without full office call required
___ generic medications optional on prescriptions

Billing Information

___ immediate payment required
___ new patient pre-payment required
___ accepts Medicaid
___ will discuss fees and charges
___ will help prepare insurance forms
___ discount for immediate cash payments

Medical Philosophy

The professional's positions on:

vitamins and nutrition _____

medical self-care _____

antibiotics _____

circumcision _____

breast feeding _____

second opinions _____

other matters _____

_____

_____

_____

_____

_____

_____

_____

Fires

Fires are the second most common cause of children's deaths.

- Install smoke alarms in all appropriate places in your home, and keep fresh batteries in them.
- Teach older children how to excape household fires, showing them the best escape routes and explaining how to avoid smoke inhalation.

Water

Drownings are the third most common children's accident.

- Begin to "waterproof" your child by giving him swimming lessons early in life. Many communities offer programs for children as young as 3 months.
- Don't leave children unattended in a tub.
- If there is water near your home, erect barriers and explain the dangers to your child. Never let your child play unattended near water, however "waterproof" she is.

Poisons

Never trust your child to avoid poison. Infants naturally explore their surroundings by putting things in their mouths, and all children are eager to ingest substances that look like pop or candy. Children also lack the taste sensibilities of adults, so they are capable of drinking a whole can of turpentine.

- Post the number of the nearest poison control center somewhere near your telephone.
- Keep syrup of Ipecac on hand to use if the poison control center recommends it.
- Stick "Mr. Yuk" labels on poisonous materials with your child's help if possible. You can get them from the National Poison Center Network, 125 DeSoto St., Pittsburgh, PA 15213, for a dollar. Mr. Yuk's* expression conveys the idea that the substance will taste awful, and that is something a child understands better than the possibility of death.

*Mr. Yuk, the poison warning symbol of the National Poison Center Network, Children's Hospital of Pittsburgh.

- Keep medicines and vitamins where children can't get them and never transfer them (or other potential poisons) to other containers. Medicines are responsible for more poisonings than any other type of substance.
- Check in these areas for products or substances that could contain poisons: under the kitchen sink, in the bathroom, in storage areas in the basement or garage, in purses (even tobacco is poisonous) or in bedside night tables. Not *all* houseplants are poisonous, but you'll have less trouble and risk if you keep them out of your child's reach.

Shocks and burns

- Cover unused outlets with nylon safety caps, meanwhile teaching your child to respect electricity.
- Protect your child against radiators, hot stoves, wood stoves, or hot cooking oil. Set your hot water heater to 110°F. to prevent scalding at the sink.
- Don't let cords to appliances, especially hot appliances, dangle where children might pull or bite them.

Falls

- Never leave your child unattended where a bad fall might occur. Keep one hand on babies on changing tables.
- Make sure all upper-story windows are secured or have secure screens.
- Teach your child to come down stairs backwards, on hands and knees.
- Install handrails at child level on all stairs that do not have them. Put child barriers or gates on stairs or doorways that pose a threat to your child.

General safety

- Remove oily rags and other fire hazards from your home.
- Examine all playthings with an eye toward ways a child might be injured by them: watch for detachable or breakable parts, small objects, splinters, jagged edges.
- Keep plastic bags away from young children.
- Store firearms unloaded, keeping ammunition carefully locked up in a separate place.

Helping Your Child Get Better

Unfortunately, kids get sick and hurt in ways you can't predict or prevent, however hard you try. This section provides information and guidelines for handling the inevitable minor—or major—ailments that come along.

Healthy Attitudes About Illness

Children are wonderful copycats but poor scholars. They learn most of their attitudes toward health not from lectures but from examples. Give some thought to the sort of example you are setting. If you respond to pain and illness in productive and sensible ways, your child will too.

Many adults need to unlearn widely held misconceptions about illness. For all the advances of medical science, there remain a great many illnesses that doctors can do nothing to cure. Being occasionally sick is part of life, especially for children who have not yet acquired the great variety of immunities adults enjoy. So it's counterproductive to regard common illnesses with resentment or alarm. After all, the only cure for many of them is time.

Parents also need to distinguish between diseases and symptoms. Coughs, sneezes, fevers, runny noses and the like are *not*

23

maladies. They are manifestations of what usually are routine illnesses. But because symptoms often interfere with an adult's employment, parents are tempted to suppress symptoms as if those symptoms in themselves are unhealthy. Often the reverse is true. For example, coughing is the body's natural way of clearing liquids or other irritants from the respiratory tract. When we attack the symptom as if it were the disease, we sometimes prolong the course of an illness. And we teach our children to overreact to what is usually a nuisance that they could otherwise cope with nicely.

The most dangerous result of this attitude is the way it teaches children to see drugs as the answer to life's problems. When parents see their child feeling miserable with some illness, they too often want to demonstrate concern and boost the child's morale by rushing to the drugstore to buy an over-the-counter (OTC) medication. When the illness eventually passes, the child naturally believes the drug made it go away. That fosters a dependent attitude toward drugs that can have a tragic consequence.

Making illness a positive experience

- Demonstrate your concern with cuddling and diversions, two remedies that have never hurt a child and that are at least as likely to promote health as drugs are.

- Don't present medicine as candy or as a total cure for the child's discomfort. Call it "medicine," and explain that it will relieve certain symptoms.

- Use the occasion of the illness to explain a little about how sickness occurs and how the body fights back. Make it clear that, although your child may feel weak, his body has marvelous resources to combat disease. Stress that it is *not* punishment for bad behavior.

Going to the doctor's office

- Don't imply that the doctor has magic powers and can produce an instant cure. Doctors don't have such powers, and they would rather not be presented as miracle workers.

- Avoid promising that doctors and nurses will not hurt your child. Shots, blood tests and other procedures *are* uncomfortable and frightening for children. Instead, tell your child that the doctor might do something mildly painful but which will speed an eventual recovery. If your child plays with dolls, you might practice "playing doctor" by giving the dolls shots which they are expected to accept with good humor.

HOW TO GET THE MOST FROM AN OFFICE CALL

This checklist will help you get more from a visit to the doctor. Think through each point as completely as you can.

Before Your Visit
1. Main reason for visit
2. Main symptoms (what, where, why, when)
3. Medicines your child is currently taking
4. What you expect the doctor will do
5. Additional matters or health concerns
6. Insurance or health-care cards and forms to take

During Your Visit
1. Name of the problem/condition (tentative? confirmed?)
2. Lab reports or diagnostic test results
3. Cause
4. Probable course of problem; time for recovery
5. How to protect others from infection (if infectious)
6. Medication (if any; is a reliable generic form available?)
7. Side effects or notes on use of medication
8. Ways to prevent recurrence of the problem
9. Date to call for lab reports (if any)
10. Date of next visit (if needed)
11. Home care (diet, activity, treatment, precautions)
12. Danger signs; reasons to call the office

Caring for a Sick Child

Many children's illnesses require a convalescence period at home. One parent or the other will need to spend time with the recovering child, ministering to his health and spirits. Contrary to what you might expect, much of what parents have heard about the care of sick children no longer seems wise to medical authorities.

- Don't automatically confine your child to bed unless you have good reason to isolate the child. There is nothing to be gained by banishing him to a remote quarter of the home or ordering bed-rest. In most cases, other family members have been amply exposed to the disease.

- Allow your convalescing child to be outdoors on pleasant days if he wishes to be. If he is dressed appropriately, there is nothing about sunshine or fresh air that will prolong his recovery period.

- Make the convalescence as pleasant as possible. Puzzles, books, coloring books, television and other diversions will make the time go quickly. But don't rely on these aids as substitutes for one of the best medicines of all—your loving attention.

DRUG USE BASICS

The following checklist will help you inform your child's doctor about drug-related conditions and ask about drugs prescribed.

What to tell the doctor

1. If your child has had allergic reactions, such as rashes, headaches or dizziness, to drugs or food taken in the past.
2. If he is taking other medicines or vitamins.
3. If he is undergoing medical treatment under the supervision of another physician.

What to ask your doctor

1. What is the name of the medicine? Write it down so you don't forget.
2. What is the medicine supposed to do? How will you know it's working?
3. What unwanted side effects might occur, such as sleepiness, swelling, nausea? Are any of them reason to call the doctor?
4. How should you administer the medicine? If you are told to give it "3 times a day," does that mean morning, noon and night? Should you give it before meals, with meals or after meals? If "every 6 hours," does that mean when your child is awake, or should you wake him up during the night to give the medicine exactly every 6 hours?
5. Are there any particular foods he should avoid while taking the medicine?
6. Should you give the medicine until it is all gone, or just until he feels better?

How to get the most from prescription drugs

1. If a drug is not doing what it is supposed to, check with your doctor. The doctor may wish to change the dosage or prescribe a different drug.
2. After you start giving the drug, if you see an unexpected symptom—such as nausea, dizziness, headache and so on—report it to your doctor immediately.
3. Read labels carefully for storage instructions. Some drugs should be kept cool and dry, others must be protected from light.
4. Never let anyone else take medication prescribed for your child, even if the symptoms seem to be the same.
5. Do not transfer medicines from the containers in which they were dispensed.
6. Do not keep prescription drugs that are no longer needed. If you have medicines left over, destroy them.

Giving medicines

It's true: "a spoonful of sugar makes the medicine go down." While you ordinarily should discourage sugar consumption, it makes sense to bend that principle slightly in order to help your sick child take the right amount of medicine.

- Crush *pills* (except time-release medications) between two tablespoons until they are a fine powder. Mix the crushed pill with jelly, applesauce, honey or something else your child likes. Have the child wash down the medicine with a sip of water or pop that's gone flat.

BABYSITTERS' MEDICAL TIPS

It pays to make sure your babysitter is as well prepared as possible to care for your child, especially if your child is sick and you must be away. When looking for a competent baby sitter, find out if she or he is familiar with first-aid and emergency procedures.

- Let the sitter know when you're making the initial arrangements that he or she will be caring for a sick child. Describe the illness and any treatment the sitter will have to give while you're gone. Make sure the sitter feels competent to take on the added responsibility.
- When the sitter arrives at your home, take time to point out the locations of medications, first aid supplies and other important items. Leave a key if these things are locked up.
- Write down the name and phone number of the place where you'll be, your doctor's name and phone number, and the time you expect to get home. (Pre-printed forms help you organize this information.*)
- Also write down any instructions you need to leave about giving medication—both timing and dosages are important. Ask your sitter to note the times when medication is given.
- Alert the sitter to any particular developments you want to hear about by phone (or any developments that warrant a call to the doctor's office).
- Call home frequently while you're gone. Doing so takes pressure off the sitter and gives you peace of mind.

*One such product, *Dear Babysitter* (Meadowbrook Press, Deephaven, MN), combines a refillable pad with a handbook for sitters, plus spaces for permanent information sitters might need.

- Don't crush capsules. They must be swallowed whole. Grease a capsule with butter, then place it far back on the tongue and have your child wash it down with liquid. Avoid choking and balking by distracting the child and making a game of drinking the liquid.
- Don't add liquid medicines to other beverages. If you do, you usually won't know if your child got the right dose. The new hollow measuring spoons sold in pharmacies make it much easier to get the right amount of liquid medicine in a child.

Fever Guide

Parents commonly think of fever as their number-one enemy when their children get sick. This leads them to battle fever aggressively with all the medication (usually aspirin or acetaminophen) and sponge baths they can give, from a mistaken

FEVER FACTS

Fever Levels

- A fever is a temperature of 100° F. orally or 100.5° F. rectally.
- The height of a fever does not correlate with the dangerousness of the disease.
- A high fever is 105° F. and above. Harmful effects of fever itself (not just discomfort) do not occur until the temperature reaches 106–107° F., and they only occur rarely. This is the highest a fever will go in people, since an automatic mechanism limits it at that point.

Fever Treatment*

- The main reason to treat a fever is to reduce your child's discomfort and the risk of dehydration.
- You don't need to treat a fever with aspirin or acetaminophen until your child's temperature goes over 102° F., and preferably only then if your child feels uncomfortable. Light clothing, extra fluids and a pleasantly cool room are better "treatments" unless the fever is higher.
- Begin sponging your child to lower his temperature only if:
  1. his temperature is over 104° F., *and*
  2. fever medications given an hour before have still not lowered his fever, *and*
  3. your child feels uncomfortable.

  If you don't wait an hour after giving medication a chance to work, your child may actually feel chilled from the sponging and the fever will rebound when you stop.
- Take your child's temperature before giving another dose of fever medication if your child is extremely hot or you are not sure he still has a fever and he's not feeling much discomfort. If your child is uncomfortable, though, it is ok to give another dose at the proper time without first checking his temperature. This way, you can track a rising fever or avoid giving medication your child doesn't need.
- If the temperature will not fall with either aspirin or acetaminophen, both may be given together, each in its usual dosage. One need not stagger the doses.
- Don't awaken your child for medication or temperature-taking. Sleep is more important than either.

When to Contact the Doctor's Office

- If your infant *less than 6 months old* has even a low fever, since he may have a serious infection without other clear-cut symptoms. (You shouldn't give fever medications to children under 1 year of age without calling the doctor's office, either.)
- If a fever without other symptoms goes over 104° F.
- If a lower fever without other symptoms lasts over 24 hours.
- If your child has a serious underlying disease and has any degree of fever.

*If your child has experienced a seizure while he had a fever, your doctor may prescribe a slightly different form of treatment when subsequent fevers occur. It's important to remember, however, that such seizures are rare, and that only a *very* small percentage of children who experience them have serious, long-lasting seizures. Finally, even for this very, very small group of children, the possibility of long-term injury from fever is nil.

HOW TO TAKE TEMPERATURES

Rectal Temperature (for children from birth to age 6)

Note: temperatures from rectal readings will be 1° higher than others.
Don't leave your child unattended while taking his temperature.

1. Shake mercury level down to below 98.6°F. (37°C.).
2. Lubricate bulb with petroleum jelly.
3. Have your child lie across your lap. Gently insert the bulb and no more than 1½ inches of the stem into his anus. Keep your hand against his bottom, to prevent injury in case he wiggles.
4. Take thermometer out after 3 minutes.
5. Wipe off thermometer and read highest level of mercury; record reading.

Oral Temperature (for children older than age 5)

Note: readings will be inaccurate if your child has had something to drink in the last 15 minutes.

1. Shake mercury level down to below 98.6°F. (37°C.).
2. Insert thermometer under his tongue.
3. Ask him to close mouth and breathe through nose.
4. Take thermometer out after 3 minutes.
5. Read highest level of mercury; record reading.

notion that the fever itself is a disease and can easily harm a child.

Fever is not a disease, however, but a symptom that shows that a fight against a disease or infection is going on inside the body. In that fight, excess heat is generated in the core of the body and is dissipated to the head and limbs, where it radiates off the skin In general, pediatricians recommend *not* trying to lower fevers under 102°F., and they certainly don't want parents to see fevers as threats to their child's well-being.

Choosing a fever medication

If your child's discomfort and temperature require more treatment than dressing him lightly and giving him lots of fluids, you need to choose between acetaminophen (e.g., Children's Anacin-3®) and aspirin. These points will help you choose wisely.

- Don't give baby aspirin to babies under 1 year of age. Use acetaminophen syrup or elixir instead, to ensure more accurate doses.

- Don't give aspirin to children with chicken pox or symptoms of influenza (fever with aches and pains, possible vomiting and possible respiratory and breathing problems). This includes children's decongestant medications that combine aspirin with other

RECOMMENDED ASPIRIN AND ACETAMINOPHEN DOSES

The table below shows how many grains (gr.) and milligrams (mg)* of aspirin or acetaminophen are recommended for children of various ages. Since forms and concentrations of these products vary, a teaspoon of syrup or a tablet made by one manufacturer may not have the same amount of medication as the same amount of another manufacturer's product. Read the label to see how concentrated the product you use is; recommended dosages should approximate those below.

Age	Medication	Amount
birth–6 months	acetaminophen (e.g., Children's Anacin-3®) only	¼ gr. (15 mg), but call the doctor before giving medication
6 months–12 months	acetaminophen only	½ gr. (30 mg), but call the doctor before giving medication
1–2 years	aspirin or acetaminophen	1 gr. (60 mg)**
2–3 years	aspirin or acetaminophen	2 gr. (120 mg)
3–4 years	aspirin or acetaminophen	3 gr. (180 mg)
4–5 years	aspirin or acetaminophen	4 gr. (240 mg)
5–8 years	aspirin or acetaminophen	6 gr. (300 mg)—1 adult tablet
8–10 years	aspirin or acetaminophen	8 gr. (400 mg)
11+ years	aspirin or acetaminophen	10 gr. (500 mg)—1 extra strength adult tablet

*Grain/milligram equivalents are approximate.
**A rule of thumb is to give 1 grain of aspirin or acetaminophen for every year of life after the first birthday, up to 10 years.

ingredients. Aspirin can upset stomachs and may be associated with development of Reye's syndrome, a potentially fatal disease (see p. 173), following its use to treat symptoms of chicken pox and influenza.

• Otherwise, aspirin and acetaminophen are both safe and about equally effective *when used properly* against fever and certain kinds of pain. Both can cause side effects and both are potentially poisonous when given in overdoses, but proper administration effectively minimizes the risk of those effects.

Dosages and overdosing

If you don't carefully measure *and* time the doses of acetaminophen (e.g., Children's Anacin-3®) or aspirin you give your child, you can overdose him. With aspirin, overdosing causes a condition called *salicylism.* Symptoms include increased irritability, vomiting, confusion, a flushed appearance, rapid breathing, and, paradoxically, a rebound fever. Prolonged aspirin overdoses can lead to skin rashes and more severe problems such as seizures, comas, and internal bleeding. Overdosing can be fatal.

With acetaminophen, overdosing is slower to show up in signs and symptoms, but it will appear as nausea, vomiting and excessive sweating. An overdose of acetaminophen can also be fatal.

If you suspect that your child has been overdosed with either aspirin or acetaminophen, call your doctor or poison control center immediately. However, if you carefully follow the guidelines on dosages below, you should never need to make such a call.

- Never give more than one dose of acetaminophen (e.g., Children's Anacin-3®) or aspirin in any 4-hour period. The medication takes effect in about 30 minutes and lasts for about 4 hours.

- Follow the label's instructions for doses, and measure the doses exactly.

Handling Emergencies

Your job in a real emergency is to calmly collect information and call for help. If you can reassure your child in the meanwhile, so much the better.

- Prepare for emergencies by posting the numbers of your doctor, the nearest poison control center, and your fire and police departments. These numbers should be on or near your phone, with other numbers that are appropriate. Take a CPR course *before* the need to use the procedure arises.

- Respond immediately to breathing emergencies, without waiting for help. Any time drowning, choking or other emergencies cause a child to stop breathing, you need to act at once (see the step-by-step instructions, pp. 71–72). If your child has choked on a solid object but *can* still breathe, keep him calm and get him to a doctor rather than attempting to remove the object yourself.

- Take the time to gather information before phoning (except in a breathing emergency). Assess the problem carefully before calling, anticipating the questions you will be asked. Typical questions cover a description of the symptoms or injury, pertinent surrounding circumstances, and supplies you may have on hand for first aid treatment.

- Try to avoid phoning for help while holding a crying child.

- Never induce vomiting without being told to do so. Some poisons

WHAT'S AN EMERGENCY?

We all recognize that there are emergencies and then there are emergencies. The conditions below are serious and require immediate medical care.

Unconsciousness   When you can't rouse a child, call for help.

Drowsiness (stupor)   When a child is conscious but unable to answer questions, get help. With infants, you may need to judge this in contrast with ordinary alertness.

Disorientation   When an older child can't remember his or her name, the place or the date (in order of decreasing importance), get help. An injury or illness causing disorientation is serious.

Severe injury   You'll know it when you see it: large wounds, obvious bone fractures and extensive burns need more care than you can give at home.

Uncontrollable bleeding   Pressure should stop most bleeding; when it fails to, get help. Children cannot afford to lose as much blood as adults.

Shortness of breath — If a child is unusually short of breath even while resting, and you can rule out hyperventilation (most common in teenagers), get help.

Severe pain   While pain is subjective, and may be caused by emotional and psychological factors, a child in intense pain still needs relief from it. Don't take pain itself as a barometer of the seriousness of the emergency, but do seek relief from a professional.

(acid, alkali and petroleum compounds) cause mouth burns or can be breathed into the lungs when vomited.

Transporting children to help

When sick or injured children must be moved to medical help, your first concern should be to reach your destination without having an accident. Accidents happen easily to parents who are distracted, concerned and driving too fast.

- Get someone to accompany you and the child if possible. The presence of a friend is reassuring, and it leaves you free to concentrate on driving. Plan your route carefully so you don't increase the chances for an accident by getting lost and panicking.

- Call for an ambulance if your child has neck or back injuries.

- Protect broken limbs or fingers against further injury. Immobilize the broken limb with homemade splints or slings, or tape the broken finger against a healthy one to keep it from moving.

- Keep the car's climate comfortable. Some parents seem to think cold night air will hurt a sick or feverish child, and so they run the heater so hot that they raise the fever.

Calming and reassuring your child

Doctors and parents alike experience the occasional frustration of finding that almost any kind of ache or pain can magically disappear by the time they get an ailing child to the clinic or emergency room. Evidently just the prospect of treatment, or the kindly reassurance of medical personnel, can have a certain curative effect. After all, pain escalates as fear increases.

In most cases, you can work some of this magic on your child. If you combine competence, calmness and comfort in your treatment, you may not make the pain disappear, but your child will probably feel better anyway.

- Be honest about the situation. It doesn't make sense to try to convince a child who's just scraped a knee that it doesn't hurt—it *does* hurt. It may help to explain what you're doing to a toddler, and for any child it may be good to remind him that the pain won't last more than a short while (but don't make false promises).
- Try distracting a child from his discomfort and pain. Cuddling, holding hands, stroking foreheads and other expressions of affection all have a place in ministering to sick and injured children, too. Deep breathing, talk about other subjects, encouraging the child to look away or to count and recite things (or to yell "ouch" if necessary) may in part block pain impulses from reaching the brain.

Special Problems

Parents have no trouble determining whether a child has a cough or fever. It is harder, though, to tell when a child has a potential handicap like impaired vision or hearing, a learning disability or some other developmental problem. It's sometimes equally hard to recognize weight problems that need special attention, or to see signs of stress and anxiety that show up as undesirable behavior or as physical complaints.

Developmental problems

Children develop physically and socially at individual rates. While certain capabilities tend to appear at certain ages, these ages vary widely from child to child. An exceptionally bright child might be mostly silent well after most infants his age have been vocalizing, then delight his parents one day by beginning to speak in complete sentences!

Though it is hard, you should be alert for developmental problems. The sooner these matters are noted and confirmed (or dismissed), the better the chances that your child will get the attention he requires. Doctors and child development specialists usually ask parents to steer a middle course between blissful ignorance and anxiety about these problems.

- Make yourself aware of child development stages (the books and groups in the Resource section will help). Pay attention to your child's vision, hearing, speech and physical development so that, if there is a problem, you'll be aware of it. Invent games that encourage your child to show and practice new skills.

- Consider that there may be physical or emotional sources for some behavioral or learning problems. A child with impaired vision or hearing may act unruly or not learn quickly because he can't see or hear directions from parents or teachers. Many children compensate for disabilities with such ingenuity that they succeed in hiding the underlying problem.

- Don't assume your child is free of problems after you've confirmed that your newborn or toddler is normal. Accidents and illnesses can sometimes cause developmental problems to appear later on.

- Feel free to ask for help. These special problems are almost never anyone's "fault," and they are far more common than once thought.

Weight problems

Your child's weight and height can be compared with national averages by using charts such as the ones on pages 230–233. Frequently, the child who seems short one year may experience a growth spurt and be quite tall for his age a year later. Deviations from national weight averages are also common, though a consistent and marked tendency toward overweight or underweight should be evaluated by your doctor.

Underweight children might be suffering from an illness such as congenital heart disease or cystic fibrosis, but it is more likely they are simply thin or small. Doctors see no value in trying to "fatten up" healthy but underweight children. When illness is the cause of underweight—which is rare—there will be other symptoms.

Obesity is more common and more troublesome. It is more likely to be the result of established patterns of eating and exercise, which will be hard to change later in life. The charts on pages 35 and 36 will help you determine what foods your child needs daily. They can guide you toward balanced diets that will help prevent obesity, yet provide for good health and growth.

DAILY NUTRITIONAL NEEDS OF INFANTS

Infants grow in irregular spurts, and their appetites vary accordingly. These guidelines will help you gauge how much your child needs to eat.

Breast Milk or Iron-Fortified Formula*

Age	Amount Per Day
Birth–1 month	18–24 oz.
1–2 months	22–26 oz.
2–3 months	24–26 oz.
3–4 months	24–28 oz.
4–5 months	24–30 oz.
5–6 months	24–32 oz.
6 months–1 year	24–32 oz.

Age	Food
Birth–4 months	Breast milk or iron-fortified infant formula
4–6 months	Breast milk or iron-fortified infant formula Baby rice cereal mixed with breast milk or formula (up to 8 tbsp.) Non-citrus juice (2–4 oz.) Strained fruits and cooked vegetables (up to 8 tbsp.)
7–9 months	Breast milk or iron-fortified infant formula Baby cereal mixed with breast milk or formula (8 tbsp.) Juice, including citrus juices (2–4 oz.) Strained to finely chopped fruits and cooked vegetables; bite-size pieces when ready (6–8 tbsp.) Strained meats and pureed egg yolks (no whites until 1 year old)
10–12 months	Breast milk or iron-fortified infant formula or vitamin D-fortified whole cow's milk (not skim or 2%) Baby cereal mixed with breast milk or formula (6–8 tbsp.) Juice (2–4 oz.) Mashed or bite-sized fruits and cooked vegetables (6–8 tbsp.) Ground or chopped meat and meat substitutes, like eggs (1–2 oz.) Potato and whole grain or enriched grain products

*If your water is not fluoridated or if it is and you are breastfeeding, you will need to supply fluoride to protect your child's teeth against decay. Adequate amounts of fluoride are not present in breast milk.

- Set a good example with your own eating and exercising habits. Children with obese parents are much more likely to have weight problems themselves and the causes are probably environmental, not hereditary.

- Resist the temptation to reward behavior with sweets. In addition to the immediate damage (tooth decay and overweight), this practice encourages unhealthy attitudes toward food that can create lifelong problems.

DAILY NUTRITIONAL NEEDS OF CHILDREN AND TEENAGERS*

Age	Bread and Cereal Group	Fruit and Vegetable Group	Milk Group	Meat Group
1-6 years	*4 servings whole grain, enriched or fortified, daily* ½–1 slice bread ¼–½ c. cooked cereal ¼–½ c. rice, noodles ½–1 oz. ready-to-eat cereal	*4 servings daily* ¼–2/3 c. juice ¼–½ c. cooked fruit ½–1 whole fruit 2–4 tbsp. vegetables	*2-3 servings daily* ½–1 c. milk ½–1 c. yogurt 1-inch cube cheese	*2 servings daily* 1 egg 2–4 tbsp. meat 2 tbsp. peanut butter 2–4 tbsp. cooked dry beans or peas
Older Children and Teenagers	*4 servings whole grain, enriched or fortified, daily* 1 slice bread ½–¾ c. cooked cereal, macaroni, noodles or rice 1 oz. ready-to-eat cereal	*4 servings daily* ½ c. cooked fruit 1 whole med. fruit ½ grapefruit 1 dinner size salad	*3-4 servings daily* 3 servings (age 7-12) 4 servings (teenagers) 1 8-oz. c. milk 1 c. yogurt 1 oz. cheddar cheese or ¾ c. milk ½ c. cottage cheese or ¼ c. milk ½ c. ice cream or 1/3 c. milk	*2 servings daily* 2–3 oz. lean meat 1 egg ½–¾ c. cooked dry beans 2 tbsp. peanut butter

*At one year of age, the average child should be eating about 1,100 calories a day. For each year after his first birthday, he should add another 100 calories (1,200 for the second year, through 2,000 for a 10-year-old). Teenage girls may need 2,400 to 2,700 calories a day, while boys of similar ages may need 3,100 to 3,600 calories a day. Remember, however, that both size and activity levels influence caloric needs.

- Suspect poor eating and exercise habits, not hormonal problems, if your child is significantly overweight.

- Look for other problems, especially problems with self-esteem and self-confidence, in obese children.

- Discuss your concerns about an overweight child with your doctor. Many parents overreact to suspected obesity, while others steadfastly refuse to acknowledge the problem when it exists.

Stress and emotional problems

Not all health problems come from obvious physical sources—viruses, bacteria, falls, cuts and so on. Some stem from emotional stresses that children inevitably encounter as they grow older. Stress is a daily fact of life for children, even infants. From the newborn upset because his mother is not able to pick him up, to the adolescent coping with the hazards of the dating game, stress is a common problem.

While the focus of this book is certainly the physical health of children, it would be inappropriate to exclude discussion of their emotional lives, especially in regard to their overall health. The subject of the effects of stress, anxiety and other emotional problems is so complex, however, that we only can treat it in the broadest of terms here.

- Seek professional help if you have any concern about your child's emotional well-being. Your pediatrician may be a good initial contact, and school social workers, family counselors, religious advisors, psychologists and other professionals may be helpful too.

- Review the resources at the end of this book for other possible assistance, and don't overlook your own friends' and relations' insight and support.

- Learn to handle your own stress effectively, and don't assume you can conceal it from your child. Trying to hide concerns your child can sense may only compound your difficulties. A simplified description of your problem—one that makes clear your child's lack of responsibility for solving it—may help.

- Anticipate especially stressful moments, like the first day at daycare or school, or a hospital visit, and prepare your child to cope with the stress. Like adults, children feel better if they feel they have a measure of control over their future activities.

Psychosomatic illnesses

It's always possible that a physical symptom may indirectly indicate a child's fears or anxieties. As Dr. T. Berry Brazelton says, "If the child needs a symptom to express his conflicts, he needs a parent's solid attention to his worries." Steering the course between overreaction and ignoring undesirable behavior (and thus not reinforcing it) is very difficult, but it is important to try to do.

- Don't make too much of habits that seem troublesome to you but that may serve important stress-reducing purposes for your child, like thumb-sucking or bedwetting. Overreacting may reinforce and prolong the behavior. Of course, the behavior itself may need your attention, but the *source* of stress that makes the behavior important to your child needs attention even more.

- Check out physical complaints, if only to rule out clearly physiological causes. Then you can gently suggest your best hunch of the emotional source of an ache, pain or habit ("I think maybe your tummy aches because you're a bit scared about starting kindergarten. Do you think there might be a lot of kids you don't know and things you won't know how to do at first?" "Maybe your head aches when you think about the problems your mom and I have in getting along together.") You might start a discussion or get a subtle sign that you were right—an abrupt change of subject, a shrug, a guarded glance. Later, talk about the problem might be possible.

- Be on the lookout for indirect physical results when your family goes through major changes or misfortunes, or when it is faced with other exceptional pressures (good and bad). Accidents, infections, and other health problems seem to crop up along with other concerns. If death, divorce or other major life events occur, take each child's different needs into account and expect different reactions (see the guide to resources at the end of this book for specific help).

Basic Supplies and Procedures

This section provides the fundamentals you need to treat your child's injuries and illnesses. In it you will find lists of the supplies you should keep on hand—safely, out of reach of your children—for first aid and routine home health care. There are also charts of baby and child anatomy, a guide to the principles of treatments, and simple how-tos for the most basic procedures—like applying compresses, bandaging and splinting. Familiarizing yourself with these charts and tables now will pay off when you need to use them later.

SUPPLIES AND EQUIPMENT CHECKLIST

Item	Use
Adhesive tape ½–1 inch wide	With gauze bandages, splints
Bandages (adhesive): assorted sizes	Cuts, scrapes
Bandages (gauze): assorted widths	Cuts, scrapes, burns
ColdHot Pack (3M)	Pain, swelling (can be reused)
Cotton balls	Applying lotions, making ear plugs
Cotton swabs	Applying lotions, cleansing
Heating pad	Pain, cramps
Hollow measuring spoon	Measuring, giving liquid medication
Hot water bottle	Pain, cramps
Ice pack	Swelling, numbing
Nasal aspirator	Nasal congestion in infants
Needles (sterilized)	Removing splinters, piercing blisters
Penlight	Examining eyes, throat
Rubbing alcohol	Cleansing skin, cooling body
Snake bite kit (where needed)	Venomous snake bites
Thermometer (oral or rectal)	Taking temperatures
Tongue depressor/Popsicle stick	Examining throat, making splints
Tweezers	Removing splinters, foreign objects

USEFUL HOUSEHOLD ITEMS

In addition to the items listed above, use household items for first aid or treatment of illnesses.

Ammonia	Salt
Baby powder	Selected foods/beverages
Baking soda	Shampoo
Belts/rope	Sheets/blankets
Cloth strips	Soap/water
Corn starch	Sticks/boards
Humidifier	Straws
Ice cubes	Towels
Knives/spoons	Toys/books
Nails/paper clips	Vaporizer
Newspaper	Vinegar
Pillows	Watch with second hand

MEDICINE CHECKLIST

Generic Name or Main Ingredient	Brand Names*	Forms	Uses
Acetaminophen (acet.)	Children's Anacin-3®	Tablet, liquid, elixir	Pain, fever
Aspirin (ASA)	—	Tablet, suppository	Pain, fever
Baby aspirin (ASA)	Bayer, St. Joseph's	Tablet	Pain, fever
Bacitracin, Neomycin (antibacterial)	Neosporin	Ointment	Cuts, wounds
Benzocaine (anesthetic)	Americaine	Ointment, spray	Topical (skin surface) pain
Calamine	—	Lotion	Poison ivy, rash
Chlorapheniramine (antihistamine)	Chlor-Trimeton	Capsule, tablet	Insect bites/stings, poison ivy, allergies
Epsom salts	—	Granules	Soaking
Guaifenesin (anti-cough)	Robitussin	Syrup	Coughs
Hydrocortisone cream	Cortaid	Cream	Rashes, itching**
Iodine (antiseptic)	Betadine	Liquid, ointment, spray	Cleaning cuts, wounds
Ipecac	—	Syrup	Poisoning (to induce vomiting)
Petroleum jelly	Vaseline	Jelly	Dry skin, blisters, taking rectal temperatures
Phenol (antiseptic)	Chloraseptic	Lozenge	Sore throat
Tolnaftate (antifungal)	Tinactin	Ointment	Fungus, athlete's foot
Zinc oxide	Desitin	Ointment	Diaper rash

*Other brands with the same generic drug ingredients may also be suitable, but get your doctor's recommendations.
**Don't use hydrocortisone creams on skin *infections*—they can spread the infection.

TREATMENT PRINCIPLES

Treatment	Examples	What it Does
Heat: dry	heating pad	Relaxes muscles
moist	warm bath	
	warm compress	Decreases inflammation, increases blood flow, increases body temperature. Can increase swelling and pain if improperly used.
Cold: moist	ice packs, cold compresses, cool baths	Relieves pain, minimizes swelling, decreases blood flow to area, lowers fever, reduces burn injury by restoring moisture and preventing extension of burn deeper into tissue, minimizes blistering, helps reduce infection.
Bandaging	gauze, adhesive bandage	Protects from infection, keeps dirt and bacteria out, promotes healing, reduces swelling, protects from further injury, holds dressings and splints in place, controls bleeding through pressure, provides support for muscles and injuries.
Splinting	for sprains, fractures	Aids healing, prevents further injury from movement; supports, immobilizes and protects parts.
Elevating	for sprains, bites, open wounds	Reduces swelling, inhibits blood flow to area, speeds clotting.
Lowering	for frostbites, fainting	Increases blood flow to area.
Pressure	to open wounds nosebleed	Controls bleeding, permits normal blood clotting to occur.
Allowing air in		Speeds formation of protective scab.
Loosening constrictions		Relieves numbness, tingling caused by a too-tight bandage, allows normal blood circulation to return, reduces chance of damage to tissue, makes breathing easier.
Slings	for upper-limb injuries	Supports injuries of the shoulder and upper extremities, immobilizes part to protect from further injury.

TREATMENTS AND PROCEDURES

Compresses

Heating pads, hot water bottles, gauze, washcloths, towels, Popsicles and ice cubes in plastic bags all can serve as compresses. Refer to the treatment principles (p. 41) or to specific entries in the treatment section (starting on p. 46) to determine what kind of compress is best for a given injury or ailment.

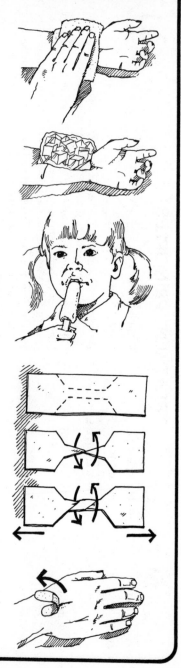

• Wet a towel or washcloth with hot or cold water; wring and fold. Or wrap an ice cube in a washcloth. Apply to face, back, joints, limbs as necessary (put in plastic bag if moisture isn't necessary).

• Apply a plastic bag filled with ice (or a Popsicle) to mouth injuries.

• Press a wad of gauze or other clean cloth to a bleeding wound and hold firmly in place to reduce flow of blood.

Bandages

Adhesive bandages, gauze pads, tape and elastic bandages help protect wounds from injury and promote healing.

• Basic bandage: stop bleeding and clean wound before applying a gauze pad or adhesive bandage (tape if needed).

• Elastic bandage: stop bleeding and apply dressings if needed, then wrap with even, *gentle* pressure. Unwrap several times a day if your doctor recommends it.

• Butterfly closure (for closing long or deep cuts): cut 1/2" adhesive tape as shown; twist one end 360° until both ends have adhesive sides down. Push edges of wound together and apply; then cover with gauze or an adhesive bandage.

• Removing bandages: leave bandages in place 24 hours unless you're directed otherwise. Then remove and change bandages as necessary. Soak gauze in cold water before removing it; remove in direction of wound (rather than across it) to avoid disturbing the scab.

Splints and Slings

Tape, string, cloth, gauze, newspaper, rulers, and boards can help to immobilize injured fingers or extremities while you seek help or allow the injury to heal. Note: don't reposition limbs that may be fractured, and don't move children with suspected neck injuries.

• Tape injured fingers or toes to adjacent ones.

• Tape or tie a ruler, board or newspaper around a broken arm or leg. Support arm with a sling or length of gauze.

• Tie towels firmly around sprained ankles, wrists.

Tourniquets

A tourniquet is a *life-saving* rather than a *limb-saving* measure. Use it to slow severe bleeding when the loss of a limb is already threatened.

1 Wrap a band of cloth twice around the injured limb just above the wound and toward the heart; don't wrap directly over a joint.

2 Tie a half-knot. Place a stick over the knot, then complete the knot to hold the stick in place.

3 Twist the stick to tighten the band until bleeding stops. Make a note of the time the tourniquet was applied and attach it to the child's clothing.

4 Seek help immediately. Don't remove the tourniquet.

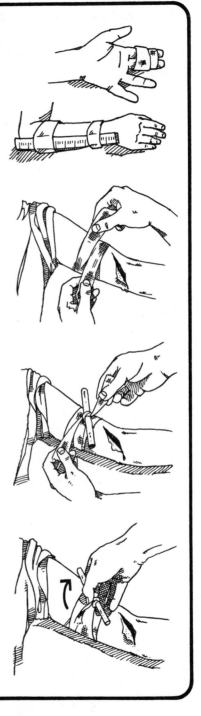

ANATOMY OF INFANTS/CHILDREN

The natural differences among the bodies of children and adults sometimes cause parents undue concern. These drawings will help you to visualize where important organs are located and to see what a normal infant looks like.

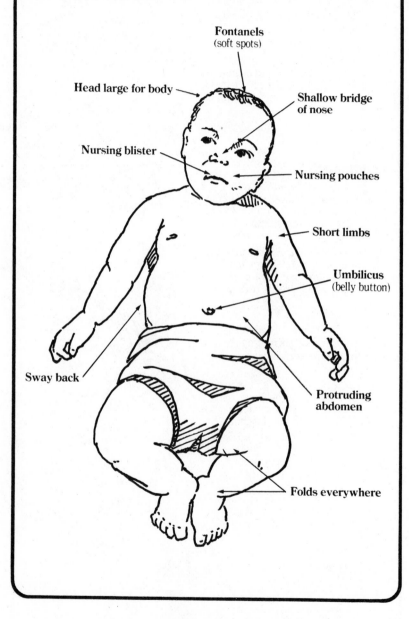

Fontanels (soft spots)

Head large for body

Shallow bridge of nose

Nursing blister

Nursing pouches

Short limbs

Umbilicus (belly button)

Sway back

Protruding abdomen

Folds everywhere

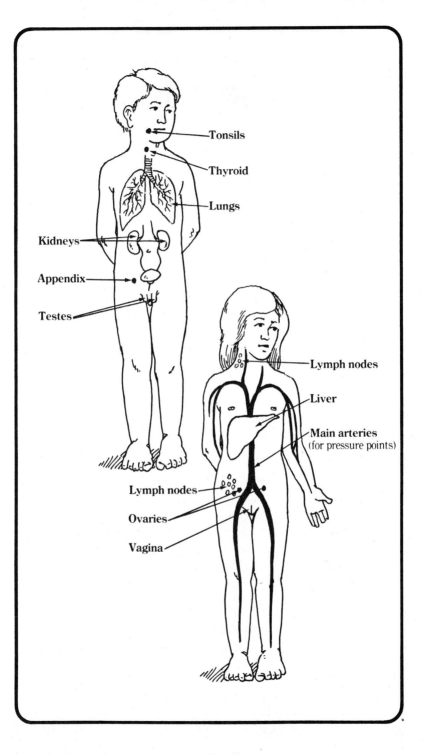

Tonsils

Thyroid

Lungs

Kidneys

Appendix

Testes

Lymph nodes

Liver

Main arteries
(for pressure points)

Lymph nodes

Ovaries

Vagina

Part 3

Step-By-Step Treatments

Introduction

When your child is sick or hurt, you want to know *quickly* what's best to do. The illustrated step-by-step treatments on the pages that follow will guide you as you care for your child, and direct you to seek professional help when that's necessary, too.

These step-by-step treatments cover the injuries, illnesses and emergencies that your child may face at one time or another while growing up. Really *rare* conditions and diseases are not included in part because professional knowledge and laboratory work are likely to be needed in diagnosing and treating them, and in part to avoid presenting you with information that is virtually certain to be useless to you. For instance, we don't cover scurvy or rickets here because they are simply not common enough to be likely complaints from your child. You won't find instructions for treating arrow wounds here, either, for the same reason.

The treatments in this section are medically sound, but they are not intended to replace professional medical care. Your own doctor may recommend other treatments for any number of reasons. Also, many illnesses vary in their symptoms and effects on different children. Your doctor will tell you that years of training will still not guarantee perfect accuracy in diagnosing and treating health problems in the office either, so it would be unrealistic to expect such accuracy, whether in your doctor's office or here. If you have any question about your child's health or the best way to handle an illness or injury, please call your doctor's office for help or advice. The following symptoms are *always* worth at least a call to your doctor's office.

WHEN TO CALL THE DOCTOR'S OFFICE

1. Any clearly life-threatening injury or accident
2. Fever (see p. 27 for guidelines)
3. Serious diarrhea
4. Blood in urine or stool
5. Sudden loss of appetite lasting 4 days or longer
6. Hoarseness, unusual crying, difficulty in breathing
7. Unusual vomiting
8. Off-color appearance; listlessness; behavior change
9. Convulsions or fits (seizures)
10. Eye or ear injuries or infections
11. Blows to head causing unconsciousness (even if brief) or having effects that last longer than 15 minutes
12. Burns with blisters; unusual rashes
13. Indications of pain (favoring a leg, wincing if a spot is touched)
14. Suspected poisoning
15. Indications of stress or anxiety
16. Swallowing a foreign body

How to use the treatment guide

For each entry that follows, you'll find a description of the subject, important background facts, tips on when to get professional help, and a list of supplies. The entries take two forms—illness entries, with symptoms, what to check and treatment blocks; and emergency/injury entries, with numbered steps for the care you can give. The samples below illustrate the two kinds of entries.

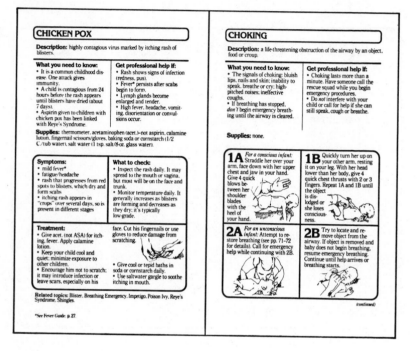

CHICKEN POX

Description: highly contagious virus marked by itching rash of blisters.

What you need to know:
• It is a common childhood disease. One attack gives immunity.
• A child is contagious from 24 hours before the rash appears until blisters have dried (about 7 days).
• Asprin given to children with chicken pox has been linked with Reye's Syndrome.

Get professional help if:
• Rash shows signs of infection (redness, pus).
• Fever* persists after scabs begin to form.
• Lymph glands become enlarged and tender.
• High fever, headache, vomiting, disorientation or convulsions occur.

Supplies: thermometer, acetaminophen (acet.)-not aspirin, calamine lotion, fingernail scissors/gloves, baking soda or cornstarch (1/2 C./tub water), salt water (1 tsp. salt/8-oz. glass water).

Symptoms:
• mild fever*
• fatigue/headache
• rash that progresses from red spots to blisters, which dry and form scabs
• itching rash appears in "crops" over several days, so is present in different stages

What to check:
• Inspect the rash daily. It may spread to the mouth or vagina, but most will be on the face and trunk.
• Monitor temperature daily. It generally increases as blisters are forming and decreases as they dry; it's typically low-grade.

Treatment:
• Give acet. (not ASA) for itching, fever. Apply calamine lotion.
• Keep your child cool and quiet; minimize exposure to other children.
• Encourage him not to scratch: it may introduce infection or leave scars, especially on his face. Cut his fingernails or use gloves to reduce damage from scratching.
• Give cool or tepid baths in soda or cornstarch baths.
• Use saltwater gargle to soothe itching in mouth.

Related topics: Blister, Breathing Emergency, Impetigo, Poison Ivy, Reye's Syndrome, Shingles.

*See Fever Guide, p. 27.

CHOKING

Description: a life-threatening obstruction of the airway by an object, food or croup.

What you need to know:
• The signals of choking: bluish lips, nails and skin; inability to speak, breathe or cry; high-pitched noises; ineffective coughs.
• If breathing has stopped, *don't* begin emergency breathing until the airway is cleared.

Get professional help if:
• Choking lasts more than a minute. Have someone call the rescue squad while you begin emergency procedures.
• Do *not* interfere with your child or call for help if she can still speak, cough or breathe.

Supplies: none.

1A *For a conscious infant:* Straddle her over your arm, face down with her upper chest and jaw in your hand. Give 4 quick blows between her shoulder blades with the heel of your hand.

1B Quickly turn her up on your other arm, resting it on your leg. With her head lower than her body, give 4 quick chest thrusts with 2 or 3 fingers. Repeat 1A and 1B until the object is dislodged or she loses consciousness.

2A *For an unconscious infant:* Attempt to restore breathing (see pp. 71-72 for details). Call for emergency help while continuing with 2B.

2B Try to locate and remove object from the airway. If object is removed and baby does not begin breathing, resume emergency breathing. Continue until help arrives or breathing starts.

(continued)

48

How to use the symptoms index

If you are perplexed about what illness your child may in fact
have, try looking up the symptoms you've noticed in the symptoms index. In reading them, see what other accompanying
symptoms match (or don't match) your child's. Then make an
educated guess about what illness your child has. Again, please
don't use the guide to "play doctor," and don't assume that every
child with mumps will have every single symptom listed in that
entry. Work closely with your doctor if you have any doubts at
all. Numbers in **boldface** refer to step-by-step entries.

SYMPTOMS INDEX

Abdominal pain 54, 102, 133, 134,
153, 168, 169, 191, **192,** 193, 201, 212
Activity levels, high **139**
Anemia **53,** 150
Appetite,
  increase in 100, 141
  loss of 54, 55, 74, 86, 133, 135, 156,
  159, 160, 171, 191, 209

Back pain 55, **58, 59,** 212
Baldness **124,** 175
Bedwetting **60,** 100, 212
Bleeding 89, 97
Blister,
  in mouth **78, 87,** 125, 135
  on body 57, **66,** 83, 125, 170
Body movement, jerking 70, **91,**
136, 174, 206
Boil **68,** 123
Bone,
  broken 59, **73**
  deformity 180
Bowel movement,
  bleeding with 150
  loss of control 91
  problems with **90,** 98, **102**
Breasts, enlarged **69**
Breathing problems 52, 53, **56, 70,**
71, 74, 75, 84, 86, 96, 98, 100, 111,
140, 168, 169, 174, 176, 184, 203, 216
Bruise 73, **76,** 150
Burn **77,** 109, 169, **196**

Chest pains 56, **82,** 168, 174
Chills 106, 115, 142, 144
Choking **84–85,** 169, 205
Confusion 89, 110, 132, 142, 169, 173
Congestion 56, 86, 106, 126
Constipation **90,** 98, 205
Convulsions **91,** 110, 169, 203

Coordination, lack of 89, 104, 129,
139, 142, 173
Cough 56, 74, 75, 86, **92,** 96, 98, 103,
144, 148, 151, 168, 206, 209, 216
Cramping 102, 130, 191,
  menstrual 153
Crying 88, 127, 200

Diarrhea 52, 98, **102,** 144, 169, 191,
192, 205
Dizziness **104,** 106, 129, 130, 136,
140, 141, 169, 211, 213
Drooling 91, 111, 135, 200
Drowsiness 99, 110, 115, 141, 142,
205

Ear,
  -ache **106,** 129, 198
  discharge from 106, 198
  object in 107
  ringing in 55, 106, 129
Eyes,
  crossed **95,** 213
  injuries to **112–114,** 213
  vision problems 95, 136, 165, 169,
  194, 211, **213**
  watery 52, 62, 86, 126, 151, 165,
  213

Fatigue 53, 83, 98, 99, 100, 130, 136,
141, 142, 144, 152, 156, 205, 209
Fever 54, 56, 67, 74, 75, 83, 86, 87,
96, 99, 103, 106, 110, **115,** 121, 125,
127, 132, 135, 137, 144, 148, 150,
151, 152, 156, 159, 160, 168, 174, 176,
177, 179, 191, 192, 193, 199, 207, 209,
212, 216

Glands,
  painful 159, 199
  swollen 67, 121, 128, 156, **159,** 179,
  188, 193, **199**

49

ACNE (NEWBORN AND ADOLESCENT)

Description: a skin condition common to newborns and adolescents that causes the skin to break out in pimples.

What you need to know:
• Newborn acne is common and cures itself.
• Acne is a common, normal condition of adolescence. It can have adverse emotional consequences and might lead to permanent skin damage, so it needs to be treated carefully.

Get professional help if:
• Your infant's acne doesn't clear in 3 days with home treatment.
• Your adolescent's acne does not respond to the recommended home treatment program.

Supplies: washcloth, soap and water, 5% or 10% benzoyl peroxide.

Symptoms:
• blackheads (pimples with dark centers)
• whiteheads (pimples with light centers)
• most often found in oily areas of the skin: around the nose, on the back, near the scalp

What to check:
• Is your adolescent daughter using greasy cosmetics?
• Is your adolescent child scratching or squeezing the pimples? This contributes to the problem.

Treatment:
• Wash your newborn's acne gently with a wet facecloth and dry. The clogged pores should open and heal by themselves without further treatment.
• Urge your child to wash frequently with mild soap and water.
• If your daughter uses makeup, be sure it is removed each night.
• Encourage your adolescent to get moderate exposure to natural sunlight. Note: sun lamps are not an effective substitute.
• Treat adolescent acne with 5% or 10% benzoyl peroxide preparations, following label directions.

ALLERGY

Description: an inherited physical reaction to pollen, dust, food and other substances.

What you need to know:
- Children with allergies are susceptible to infections.
- Symptoms vary, depending on the child's age and emotional status and the season.
- Tobacco smoke worsens allergic respiratory symptoms.

Get professional help if:
- Symptoms of allergy are present without other symptoms of illness. Lab tests may be done to identify allergens.
- A reaction is severe (difficulty breathing, shock).
- Severe swelling develops.

Supplies: penlight, OTC antihistamines (chlorpheniramine), prescribed medications.

Symptoms:
- watery eyes/runny nose
- itching skin/rash
- hives
- tingling lips and tongue
- itchy throat/swollen lips
- diarrhea
- nausea/vomiting
- dark circles under eyes
- trouble breathing

What to check:
- With a penlight, examine nasal membranes for pale, swollen surfaces.
- Look for dark circles under the child's eyes.
- Has child eaten any new foods or handled any new plants, textiles or chemicals? List possible irritants.

Treatment:
- Allergies should be diagnosed by a doctor to determine a treatment plan, which will depend on the allergy.
- Give medications as prescribed or recommended by your doctor.
- Eliminate allergens (infants allergic to cow's milk can be given soybean substitute; contact with irritating soaps, wool can be avoided; home and child's room can be kept free of dust).

Related topics: Asthma, Bronchiolitis, Bronchitis, Croup, Hay Fever, Hives.

ANEMIA

Description: a shortage of hemoglobin (an iron- and oxygen-carrying substance) in the blood.

What you need to know:

• There are many types of anemia. The most common is an iron deficiency caused by poor diet.
• Sickle-cell anemia is hereditary among Blacks and people of Mediterranean descent.

Get professional help if:

• Symptoms make you suspect anemia. A variety of laboratory tests is required to identify the presence and type of anemia; a doctor's help is necessary to ensure proper diagnosis and treatment.

Supplies: none.

Symptoms:

• chronic weakness, tiredness, irritability
• paleness of lips or fingernails
• shortness of breath
• rapid pulse

What to check:

• Is your child's diet balanced and nutritionally sound?
• Does one family member have anemia? If so, watch for symptoms in others.

Treatment:

• Do *not* attempt home remedies.
• A doctor's treatment will vary, depending on the type and severity of anemia. It may include blood tests and then supplements of iron, vitamin B_{12} and folic acid. Blood transfusions may be needed if anemia results from excessive bleeding.

Related topics: Jaundice in Newborns, Nosebleed.

APPENDICITIS

Description: an inflammation of the appendix that causes pain in the abdominal area.

What you need to know:
• Appendicitis is difficult to diagnose because abdominal pain is associated with many other conditions.
• It is common but serious.
• The appendix is attached to the large intestine and has no known use.

Get professional help if:
• Pain in abdomen persists for more than 3 hours. (Inflammation progresses rapidly and may cause the organ to burst, spreading infection to the entire abdominal area.)

Supplies: thermometer.

Symptoms:
• constant pain that usually begins in the area of the navel and moves to the lower-right abdomen
• temperature of 100–101°F.*
• loss of appetite
• nausea/vomiting

What to check:
• Is the lower-right area of abdomen tender?
• Are there indications of a condition other than appendicitis (see related topics)?

Treatment:
• Since stomach pain most often indicates ailments other than appendicitis, don't be overly concerned at first.
• Monitor temperature and pain every 2 hours.
• Do *not* give laxatives.
• If pain persists, contact your physician. While there are no conclusive tests to diagnose appendicitis, tests for infection can indicate its likelihood.
• Treatment usually involves surgical removal of the organ.

Related topics: Constipation, Stomach Flu, Stomach Pain.

*See Fever Guide, p. 27.

ARTHRITIS

Description: stiffness and inflammation of any joint, particularly joints that are used frequently.

What you need to know:	Get professional help if:
• This treatment plan is for use only after your child has been diagnosed. • Some arthritic conditions are more crippling than others.	• You suspect your child has arthritis. • A joint is red, swollen, and movement is limited. • Stomach pain, vomiting, sore throat or a severe puncture wound is present; get help immediately. • Joint pain with fever* lasts more than a day.

Supplies: thermometer; heating pad, hot water bottle or ColdHot Pack (3M); aspirin (ASA)—*not* acetaminophen (acet.)—*if* recommended by a doctor.

Symptoms:	What to check:
• aching joints • bumps in and around joints • stiff wrist, shoulder, neck • limping, difficulty walking • back, knee, hip pain • intermittent pain • ringing in ear • loss of appetite	• Note the time of day when the aching is worst. • Are there any symptoms that indicate injury or any other illness (see related topics)?

Treatment:
• Do not treat for arthritis until it has been diagnosed by a doctor. If pain occurs suddenly, treat as a limb injury until you can see a doctor. Treatment might include:
-applying heat
-massaging muscles surrounding sore joint
-dressing your child warmly
-making sure he gets enough exercise to maintain muscle strength, followed by rest
-giving ASA (not acet.) for discomfort.

Related topics: Cut/Wound, German Measles, Sore Muscle, Sprain.

*See Fever Guide, p. 27.

ASTHMA

Description: a lung condition in which linings of bronchial tubes are inflamed, swollen, clogged with mucus; surrounding muscles are tight.

What you need to know:
- Asthma distress can be frightening. Calmness and reassurance may reduce the severity of an attack.
- Causes include viruses, dust, pollen, food, reaction to medication, dampness, temperature change, emotional stress, fatigue, pets and feathers.

Get professional help if:
- It is his first attack. A professional can determine the cause and treat the condition.
- Congestion makes him unable to eat, drink, sleep.
- Sputum changes from white to yellow, green, grey, red.
- Vomiting occurs more than twice in a few hours.

Supplies: thermometer; pillows; liquids; OTC or prescribed asthma medications; toys, books, etc. to distract your child.

Symptoms:
- labored breathing
- difficulty exhaling
- wheezing/whistling
- shortness of breath
- aching in chest
- difficulty sleeping
- fever*
- congestion/runny nose
- coughing/sneezing

What to check:
- Note all possible irritants.
- Does your child have trouble breathing when lying down? If so, prop him up with pillows.

Treatment:
- Keep your child quiet and distracted during an attack.
- Offer room temperature liquids frequently.
- Follow treatment plan prescribed by your doctor. It may include:

–OTC or prescribed asthma medication
–shots to build resistance to allergies
–breathing exercises
–special measures to keep your home free of allergens (e.g., tobacco smoke).

Related topics: Allergy, Bronchiolitis, Croup, Hay Fever.

*See Fever Guide, p. 27.

ATHLETE'S FOOT

Description: fungus-caused infection of skin on the feet, especially between the third and fourth toes.

What you need to know:
- Athlete's foot is very common in adolescents, rare in younger children.
- It is aggravated by heat, sweating, rubbing of skin.
- The fungus is picked up at pools, gyms, showers.

Get professional help if:
- The condition is severe (spread to toenails, bottom of feet, ankles).
- Home remedies do not ease symptoms.

Supplies: tolnaftate (antifungal) foot powder or ointment (*not* hydro-cortisone cream).

Symptoms:
- itching
- redness, scaling of skin between toes
- blisters and unpleasant odor

What to check:
- Are feet dried thoroughly after washing?
- Socks should be clean, shoes dry.

Treatment:
- Wash the child's feet twice daily and apply powder or ointment.
- Change her socks twice daily, more often if there is excessive sweating.
- Dress her in sandals or cotton socks and well-ventilated shoes; avoid rubber soles and plastic linings in shoes.
- If the condition is severe, keep her off her feet as much as possible.

Related topics: Blister, Eczema, Poison Ivy, Ringworm.

BACKACHE

Description: soreness resulting from stress on back muscles and ligaments.

What you need to know:	Get professional help if:
• Most backaches result from overexertion. • Severe or localized pain may indicate a more serious problem—kidney infection, skeletal deformity, bone fracture or pressure on nerve.	• Pain is severe, localized, or extending down one leg. • There is fever* or a urinary problem. • Legs are weak. • Home treatment does not improve the condition within 24 hours.

Supplies: heating pad, aspirin (ASA)/acetaminophen (acet.), thermometer, firm mattress, pillows, towel.

Symptoms:
• soreness of back muscles, often those of the lower back.

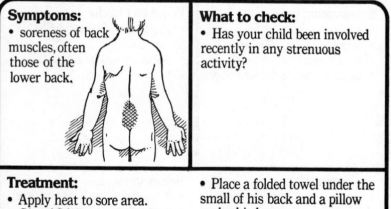

What to check:
• Has your child been involved recently in any strenuous activity?

Treatment:
• Apply heat to sore area.
• Give ASA/acet. every 4 hours for pain. Monitor temperature.
• Have your child flat on his back as much as possible.

• Place a folded towel under the small of his back and a pillow under his knees.
• Increase activity gradually.

Related topics: Back or Neck Injury, Urinary Tract Infection.

*See Fever Guide, p. 27.

BACK OR NECK INJURY

Description: possible fracture of the back or neck, often caused by a blow or fall.

What you need to know:

• Unless it is absolutely necessary, don't attempt to move your child if you suspect her back or neck is broken.
• If your child *must* be moved, get several people to help. Turn the entire body as a unit, keeping it as stable as possible.

Get professional help if:

• You suspect your child's back or neck is fractured.
• Your child complains of persistent back pain and has difficulty bending forward and backward.
• Bleeding from an associated cut or wound is excessive.

Supplies: rolled-up towels or clothing, board and belts, rope.

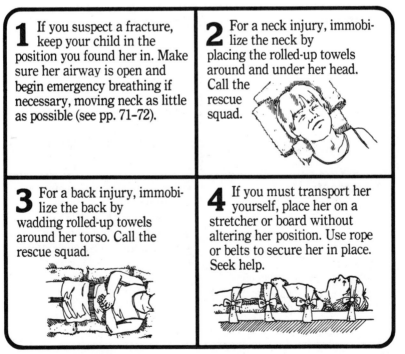

1 If you suspect a fracture, keep your child in the position you found her in. Make sure her airway is open and begin emergency breathing if necessary, moving neck as little as possible (see pp. 71-72).

2 For a neck injury, immobilize the neck by placing the rolled-up towels around and under her head. Call the rescue squad.

3 For a back injury, immobilize the back by wadding rolled-up towels around her torso. Call the rescue squad.

4 If you must transport her yourself, place her on a stretcher or board without altering her position. Use rope or belts to secure her in place. Seek help.

Related topics: Backache, Sprain.

BEDWETTING

Description: failure to control the bladder during sleep.

What you need to know:
• Bedwetting is an unconscious, not a deliberate, act.
• Many children wet their beds occasionally through ages 6 or 7, especially after stressful or exciting events.

Get professional help if:
• There is fever,* stomach pain, frequent or painful urination, or blood in the urine.
• Your child has difficulty controlling his bladder during the day as well as at night.
• Bedwetting occurs continuously beyond age 5 or begins after several months of dryness.

Supplies: thermometer, prescribed medication, gold stars to place on chart or calendar, rubber pad with extra sheet on top, commercial bedwetting alarm system.

Symptoms:
• consistent failure to remain dry throughout the night

What to check:
• Is your child drinking an excessive amount of fluid in the evening?
• Could he be under stress from a change in environment (such as moving, a new family member)?
• Are there signs of urinary infection? Constipation?

Treatment:
• Act confident in his ability to control bedwetting in time.
• Reward successful behavior by placing stars on a chart or calendar.
• Place a rubber pad covered with an extra sheet over the regular sheet to protect the mattress.

• Try a bedwetting alarm (use according to instructions).
• *Do not* punish a child or let others make him feel guilty.
• *Don't* overemphasize daytime training.

Related topics: Diabetes, Urinary Tract Infection.

*See Fever Guide, p. 27.

BIRTHMARK

Description: a discoloration or raised area on the skin; very common and almost always harmless.

What you need to know:
- Some birthmarks are clusters of small blood vessels on or under the skin (hemangiomas).
- Some marks are present at birth, while others develop in the first months of life.
- Most birthmarks disappear on their own by school age.

Get professional help if:
- A birthmark grows abnormally fast.
- There is redness of surrounding skin, discharge or odor.
- A raised mark is located on a part of the body where it is repeatedly bumped and irritated.
- A port wine stain shows noticeably on the face.

Supplies: none.

SIGNS:

Strawberry Mark: • a flat or raised red mark shaped like a strawberry • usually grows darker for a period of months, then gradually disappears • is more common in girls than in boys	*Salmon Patch (stork bite):* • a cluster of small, red spots • usually appears on the back of the neck, upper eyelid or bridge of nose • usually disappears
Mongolian Spot: • a bluish spot that resembles a bruise • often found on the lower back or buttocks • most commonly found on brunettes and among dark-complected people • usually disappears	*Port Wine Stain:* • a reddish patch • frequently appears on the forehead • more common on blondes than brunettes • usually fades somewhat but does not disappear

BITES AND STINGS, INSECT

Description: a painful welt or burning sensation in reaction to an insect bite or wasp, bee or hornet sting.

What you need to know:

- Severe, *generalized* allergic reactions are rare, but can be fatal.
- Usually the pain, itching and welt are *localized* and subside in 3–4 hours.
- Keeping your child quiet will keep the venom from spreading and minimize the reaction.

Get professional help if:

- You see signs of severe allergic reaction: swollen, itchy eyes; wheezing; clammy, bluish skin; abdominal cramps; nausea.
- Your family has a history of allergic reaction to stings.
- There are multiple stings.

Supplies: knife blade, soap and water, ice, baking soda/ammonia paste *or* calamine lotion *or* vinegar, aspirin (ASA)/acetaminophen (acet.).

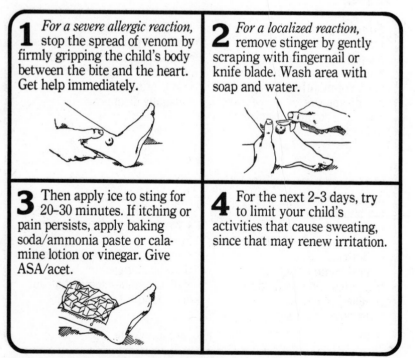

1 *For a severe allergic reaction,* stop the spread of venom by firmly gripping the child's body between the bite and the heart. Get help immediately.

2 *For a localized reaction,* remove stinger by gently scraping with fingernail or knife blade. Wash area with soap and water.

3 Then apply ice to sting for 20–30 minutes. If itching or pain persists, apply baking soda/ammonia paste or calamine lotion or vinegar. Give ASA/acet.

4 For the next 2–3 days, try to limit your child's activities that cause sweating, since that may renew irritation.

Related topics: Allergy, Hives, Rocky Mountain Spotted Fever (for removing ticks).

BITES, ANIMAL AND HUMAN

Description: bites by humans, pets and animals such as skunks, raccoons, etc.

What you need to know:
- Because the mouths of humans and animals contain many kinds of bacteria, a bite that deeply punctures the skin is likely to result in infection, possibly tetanus.
- While rabies rarely develops, it is a possibility.

Get professional help if:
- Bleeding is severe.
- The animal acts rabid, is known not to be currently vaccinated against rabies, or is a skunk or fox.
- Infection (redness, swelling, pain, fever,* irritability, fatigue) appears within 7 days.
- DPT immunization isn't current.

Supplies: soap and water, antiseptic, sterile bandage, prescribed medication (often antibiotics), thermometer.

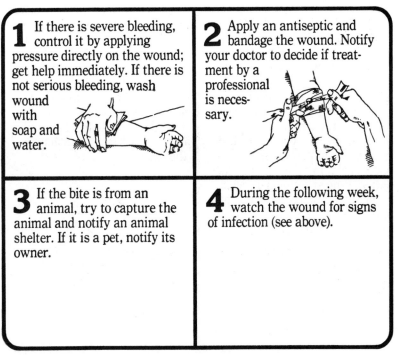

1 If there is severe bleeding, control it by applying pressure directly on the wound; get help immediately. If there is not serious bleeding, wash wound with soap and water.

2 Apply an antiseptic and bandage the wound. Notify your doctor to decide if treatment by a professional is necessary.

3 If the bite is from an animal, try to capture the animal and notify an animal shelter. If it is a pet, notify its owner.

4 During the following week, watch the wound for signs of infection (see above).

Related topics: Cut/Wound, Tetanus.

*See Fever Guide, p. 27.

BITES, POISONOUS SNAKES

Description: introduction of poisonous venom to the bloodstream by pit vipers and coral snakes.

What you need to know:

• The bite of a poisonous snake is distinguished from a non-poisonous bite by the presence of 1 or more fang marks in the skin.
• *Don't* give aspirin, sedatives or alcohol to a child bitten by a snake.

Get professional help if:

• Your child has been bitten by a poisonous snake.
• All poisonous snake bites require medical help. Closely monitor the reaction; apply home treatment on the way to the doctor.

Supplies: strips of cloth 3/4–1 1/2 in. wide, alcohol, snake-bite kit *or* knife *or* razor blade, soap and water, bandage, washcloth.

1 Seek help immediately if you think the snake is poisonous. Try to identify the snake; kill it and bring it with you to the doctor if possible. Otherwise, keep child quiet and calm to limit the spread of venom. Have him lie down; immobilize the part of his body that was bitten. Reassure and comfort him. Monitor the reaction. If no symptoms develop, no further home treatment is required.

2 If intense pain, swelling or skin discoloration develop, apply a constricting band 2–4 inches above the fang marks, but below the level of the heart (you should be able to slip a finger between the band and the skin). Loosen the band if swelling makes it too tight. Monitor the reaction.

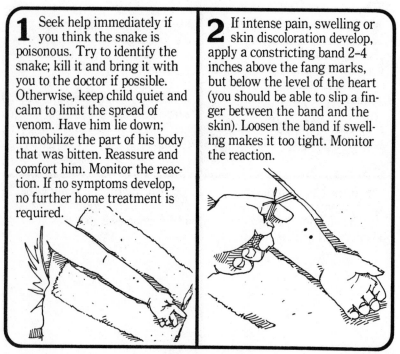

(continued)

3 If weakness, rapid pulse, nausea, dimmed vision develop in the first 30–60 minutes and medical help isn't available, clean the area of the bite with alcohol. Make shallow 1 1/2-inch-long cuts through the fang marks with a sterile knife. Suck out the venom with your mouth or a suction cup from a snake-bite kit; spit out the venom.

4 If skin above the band begins to swell, apply a second band above the swollen area; loosen but don't remove the first band. Wash the wound with soap and water, blot dry, apply a bandage. Cover it with a cold, wet cloth. Watch for signs of shock; give artificial respiration if necessary (see pp. 71-72).

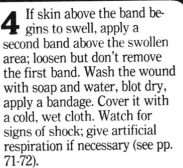

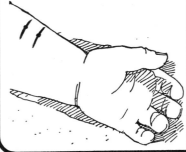

Related topics: Shock.

BLISTER

Description: an accumulation of fluid between layers of skin.

What you need to know:
• Can be caused by friction (such as from a shoe rubbing a heel), burns, infection, allergic reaction, viruses, funguses.
• It usually is best not to break blisters—they heal themselves in 3-4 days.

Get professional help if:
• Blister shows pus.
• Red streaks extend outward from blister.
• Surrounding skin becomes, red, swollen or tender.
• Blister is due to a burn.

Supplies: sterile needle or straight pin, gauze bandage, petroleum jelly.

Symptoms:
• appearance of fluid under a raised layer of skin

What to check:
• Watch for signs of infection.
• Are other symptoms (such as rash or itching) present that may indicate chicken pox, athlete's foot, poison ivy or some other condition?

Treatment:
• If blister is large or in an uncomfortable location, clean it, puncture it at the base with a sterile needle, and drain off the fluid. Bandage.
• If blister is broken, cover with a gauze bandage; put petroleum jelly on bandage to prevent it from sticking to the skin.

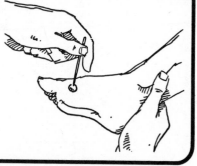

Related topics: Athlete's Foot; Burn; Chicken Pox; Cold Sore/Fever Blister; Hand, Foot and Mouth Disease; Herpes Stomatitis; Poison Ivy.

BLOOD POISONING

Description: infection of the skin, lymph vessels and lymph nodes by bacteria, a condition better termed lymphangitis.

What you need to know:
- It results from spread of infection from a wound (such as a cut or blister) to the lymph vessels and lymph nodes ("glands").
- If neglected for several days, the bacteria can reach the bloodstream and cause a severe, generalized infection.

Get professional help if:
- Fever is greater than 101°F.*
- Red streaks extend from the wound.
- Pus is draining from the wound.

Supplies: aspirin (ASA)/acetaminophen (acet.), 1/2 c. Dreft detergent in 1 qt. very warm (not hot) water, sterile needle.

Symptoms:
- fever*
- red streaks extending from wound
- red, swollen, tender lymph nodes near affected area

What to check:
- If fever is lower than 101°F.* and lymph nodes aren't seriously affected, apply home treatment to reduce the infection.

Treatment:
- There is no home treatement for blood poisoning. However, you can treat an *infected wound* at home with these steps:
-Elevate the affected area.
-Give ASA/acet. to relieve pain.
-Soak wound in Dreft detergent solution.
-If wound has an infected blister, open it with a sterile needle and drain the pus. Watch for spread of infection. Get help if it spreads.

Related topics: Blister, Boil, Creeping Eruption, Cut/Wound.

*See Fever Guide, p. 27.

BOIL

Description: a localized skin infection characterized by a painful skin abcess (collection of pus).

What you need to know:

• Infection is caused when bacteria (usually staphylococcus) enters a skin break.
• When pus drains from a broken boil, infection may spread to other parts of the body, or even to other people.

Get professional help if:

• A boil is located on the face.
• Fever, red streaks, or more boils develop.
• The abcess does not break and drain on its own in a week.
• The infection does not subside after the boil breaks.

Supplies: hot compresses, soap and water, solution of 1/2 c. Dreft detergent in 1 qt. water, sterile bandages, antibiotics.

Symptoms:

• painful red bump with a white center
• white center grows, forms a head, breaks and drains pus in 4–7 days

What to check:

• Are there signs of serious or spreading infection?
• Watch for boil to break and drain; home treatment is important at this stage.

Treatment:

• *Do not* force a boil open by squeezing or puncturing it; this may spread infection.
• Apply hot compresses.
• Wash the affected area frequently with soap and water.
• Soak twice daily in Epsom salt or Dreft solution.
• After the boil breaks, continue applying hot compresses; express the pus and apply sterile bandages.
• If the infection is persistent a doctor may prescribe antibiotics.

Related topics: Blister, Blood Poisoning.

BREAST ENLARGEMENT

Description: a temporary enlargement of breasts in infants or adolescent males.

What you need to know:
• Infants, including males, receive hormones from the mother across the placenta that can cause enlarged breasts in a newborn.
• About 50 percent of adolescent males experience enlargement of one or both breasts during puberty.

Get professional help if:
• The enlargement of your adolescent son's breasts is pronounced, lasts more than a year or is a source of embarrassment. Cosmetic surgery is a possible cure, though it is rarely needed or done.

Supplies: none.

Symptoms:
• enlarged breasts

What to check:
• Are your adolescent son's breasts unusually enlarged?

Treatment:
• No treatment is necessary for infants with enlarged breasts.
• The swelling usually disappears within 4 weeks of birth because the newborn is then no longer receiving hormones from the mother.
• No treatment is necessary for adolescent males with enlarged breasts except in rare cases. The condition usually disappears within a year, and should not be cause for concern.

BREATH-HOLDING

Description: an inability to regain breath, usually during a temper tantrum or after a fall; often preceded by angry, hard crying.

What you need to know:

• Unlike breathing emergencies or choking, this is *not* a life-threatening event.
• Your ability to react matter-of-factly will help deter your child from future breath-holding.
• Unconscious and jerky limbs that may follow breath-holding cause no injury.

Supplies: none.

Get professional help if:

• Your child develops a habit of breath-holding in response to anger or fear.
• Your child falls unconscious and automatic breathing is not immediately restored. Begin emergency breathing while someone calls for help (see p. 71–72).

Symptoms:

• reddened face
• ability to breathe or cry up to the moment of breath-holding
• inability to draw in breath after a long wail
• sometimes, unconsciousness, slightly bluish face and limb-jerking

What to check:

• Does your child begin to breathe immediately if she falls unconscious? If not, get help and begin emergency breathing.
• Is the breath-holding becoming habitual?

Treatment:

• Treat it as a symptom of a tantrum unless it's from a fall. Try to ignore it.
• If she passes out during a breath-holding spell, let her lie comfortably until spontaneous breathing brings her to consciousness.

• Act casual about the incident, even though you may be concerned.

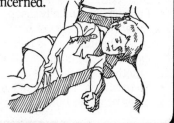

Related topics: Convulsion, Unconsciousness.

BREATHING EMERGENCY

Description: a life-threatening situation resulting from a blocked airway, electric shock or other condition.

What you need to know:
• Act quickly while someone calls for emergency help. Procedures vary with child's age.
• If *choking* is the cause, follow the procedures on p. 84 to dislodge the object. Then begin emergency breathing if needed.
• Don't tilt head if you suspect a back or neck injury.

Get professional help if:
• A child's breathing stops. Follow the procedures below until emergency help arrives.

Supplies: none.

1 *Begin while help is coming.* Clear the airway. Place child on back, tilt head to point chin up. Listen for breathing. Clear mouth gently with fingers.

2A *For an infant,* cover the mouth *and* nostrils with your mouth and give 4 quick puffs. If he still is not breathing, give one breath every 4 seconds.

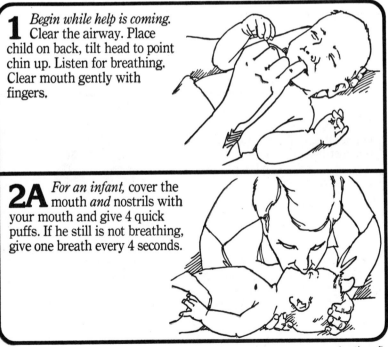

(continued)

2B *For a child aged 1-8,* cover mouth *and* nostrils with your mouth. Give 4 quick puffs. If he still is not breathing, give 1 breath every 4 seconds.

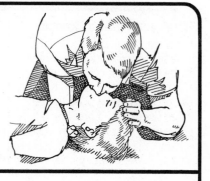

2C *For a child older than 8,* give 4 quick puffs into mouth only, closing the nose by squeezing the nostrils between thumb and index finger. If he still is not breathing, give 1 breath every 5 seconds.

3 *Continue to breathe for the child.* If these procedures do not seem to restore breathing, readjust head tilt to open airway and continue to breathe until help arrives.

Related topics: Cardiac Arrest, Choking, Croup, Drowning, Epiglottitis, Swallowed Object.

BROKEN BONE (FRACTURE)

Description: a crack or break in a bone that causes pain, swelling, bruising and sometimes bone deformity.

What you need to know:
• A child's broken bone usually heals faster and more easily than an adult's.
• Some breaks may not be readily detected, particularly crushed vertebrae or wrist and ankle breaks.

Get professional help if:
• You suspect back or neck fractures.
• An injured limb is deformed, cold, blue, numb or swells rapidly.
• The child cannot bear weight on a limb, mobility is reduced, or the child complains of persistent pain.

Supplies: bandage, splint or slings, aspirin (ASA)/acetaminophen (acet.).

1 *Never* move a child whose back or neck may be broken unless absolutely necessary. Gently touch the injured area to see if it causes pain. If a bone is crooked or deformed, don't try to force it into place.

2 If there is an open wound, treat for bleeding (see p. 97). Apply a bandage, moving the limb as little as possible.

3 Immobilize the injured limb by applying a splint or sling (see p. 43). Give ASA/acet. for pain.

4 Get professional help. Keep your child warm and observe for shock (see p. 184). Don't give anything to eat or drink in case anesthesia is needed.

Related topics: Back or Neck Injury, Chest Pain, Cut/Wound, Knee Pain, Nose Injury.

BRONCHIOLITIS

Description: inflammation and constriction of the smallest air passages (bronchioles) due to viral infection.

What you need to know:
- Bronchiolitis occurs mostly in infants.
- It has many of the same symptoms as asthma and pneumonia.
- It usually lasts several days, but will resolve by itself.

Get professional help if:
- Symptoms are present, if only to be sure it's bronchiolitis.
- Your baby's lips or skin appear blue or your infant seems to be tiring from the increased effort to breathe.
- Your infant refuses fluids for a day, or vomits what he drinks.

Supplies: thermometer, prescribed medication, liquids, cool mist vaporizer.

Symptoms:
- rapid, shallow breathing
- labored breathing
- wheezing
- fever*
- cough
- loss of appetite

What to check:
- Note temperature 3 times daily.

Treatment:
- Follow treatment recommended by your doctor. It probably will include these:
-prescribed medication
-frequent clear liquids
-humidifying the air.

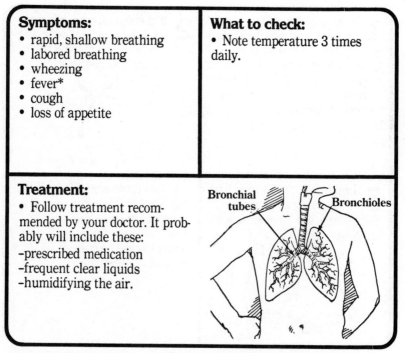

Bronchial tubes   Bronchioles

Related topics: Allergy, Asthma, Bronchitis, Cold, Pneumonia.

*See Fever Guide, p. 27.

BRONCHITIS

Description: inflammation of the airways (bronchial tubes), caused by bacteria or viral infection.

What you need to know:
- Typically, it is preceded by an upper respiratory infection.
- It is contagious.
- Untreated, chronic bronchitis can lead to lung disease.
- It has many of the same symptoms as pneumonia and cough.

Get professional help if:
- Coughing persists.
- Temperature is over 101°F. several times in one day.*
- An infant coughs often.
- The respiration rate is over 20/minute for a child and 40/minute for an infant.

Supplies: thermometer, watch with second hand, liquids, aspirin (ASA)/acetaminophen (acet.), cool mist vaporizer, cough medicine (expectorant type).

Symptoms:
- labored breathing
- wheezing
- burning in chest
- fever*
- dry, hacking cough that changes to wet cough, then back to dry cough
- bad breath
- runny nose

What to check:
- Note temperature 3 times a day.
- Note the color of sputum. It usually changes from clear to greenish-yellow to clear. (Yellow, green or brown sputum may indicate a bacterial infection, which may require an antibiotic).

Treatment:
- Keep your child quiet and resting. Minimize contact with other people.
- Offer liquids frequently.
- Give ASA if fever is present.
- Humidify air with cool vapor.
- Use postural drainage technique twice daily if your doctor recommends it.

Related topics: Allergy, Asthma, Bronchiolitis, Cold, Croup, Whooping Cough.

*See Fever Guide, p. 27.

BRUISE

Description: visible mark near the skin surface that indicates bleeding from broken blood vessels.

What you need to know:
• Most bruises result from a blow.
• Children with fair complexions show bruises more easily than those with dark complexions.
• It generally takes 2 weeks for a bruise to disappear completely.

Get professional help if:
• Bruises appear spontaneously, without apparent injury.
• There are signs of a bone break, such as a deformed limb or impaired movement.
• Bruises form easily or are more serious than it seems the injuries warrant.

Supplies: ColdHot Pack (3M), heating pad (optional).

Symptoms:
• maroon, purple, green or yellow mark on the skin (it may be any size)

What to check:
• Determine the cause of a bruise—a fall, bump, etc.
• Is there a cut or deformity?

Treatment:
• Minor bruises may not require treatment. Most bruises are maroon or purple as new injuries, then turn green or yellow as blood is resorbed.

• With a more serious injury, application of a cold pack for 12–24 hours may minimize bruising.
• After 24 hours, heat may speed disappearance of the bruise.

Related topics: Broken Bone (Fracture), Cut/Wound, Sprain.

BURN

Description: an injury resulting from heat, hot liquids, electrical shock, chemicals or radiation.

What you need to know:

• First-degree burns redden the skin. Second-degree burns cause tissue injury that allows fluid to accumulate under the skin and form a blister. Third-degree burns involve burning of the skin tissue.
• Burns that cover more than 10% of the body may require hospitalization.

Get professional help if:

• Burn covers more than 10% of body surface or is on the face.
• Areas of brown or blackened skin are evident (third-degree burn).
• Healing does not occur in a week or persistent pain isn't relieved with aspirin.
• There are signs of infection (swelling, pus, redness).

Supplies: clean cloth, cold water or ice, mild soap, prescribed burn ointment or petroleum jelly, gauze dressing, tape.

1 If burn is *serious* or *extensive,* keep your child lying down, remove his clothing (unless it sticks to the skin), and cover the burn with a clean cloth. Keep him warm and seek help. Do *not* apply dressings or oil-based substances to severe burns.

2 If burn is less serious, apply cold water or ice for 1 hour, washing with mild soap.

3 Then apply burn ointment or petroleum jelly (never butter or grease, which may cause infection). Cover with sterile dressing taped loosely in place. Elevate burn to aid drainage; keep it motionless to help healing. Bedrest may be needed for foot and leg burns.

4 Change dressing daily. To remove dressing, rinse with lots of cold water. Don't break blisters, but do remove dead skin if it's not part of an intact blister.

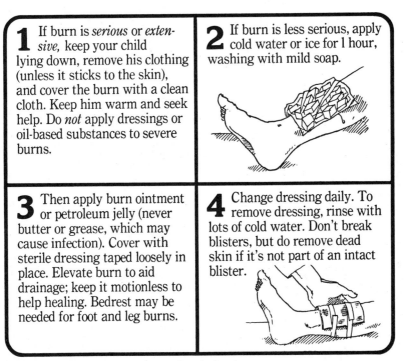

Related topics: Blister, Electric Shock, Sunburn.

CANKER SORE

Description: blisters or sores in the mouth caused by several types of viruses.

What you need to know:	Get professional help if:
• Canker sores are not caused by herpes viruses. • Unlike other mouth sores, canker sores are not related to fever, stress or other such conditions.	• Canker sores recur several times in a few months, or are particularly painful.

Supplies: penlight, thermometer.

Symptoms:	What to check:
• one or a few blisters in the mouth, with mild or no pain	• Using a penlight, check inside the child's mouth. Are there few or many blisters? • Is there pain? • Has the child had a fever* or recently been under stress? If so, the sores might be fever blisters or herpes stomatitis.

Treatment:
• Canker sores usually require no treatment.

Related topics: Cold Sore/Fever Blister; Hand, Foot and Mouth Disease; Herpes Stomatitis.

*See Fever Guide, p. 27.

CARDIAC ARREST

Description: a life-threatening condition when the heart stops due to breathing emergency or other situation.

What you need to know:
• Know the A-B-C of cardio-pulmonary resuscitation (CPR): *Airway, Breathing, Circulation.* Get CPR training *before* you need to use it.
• If choking is the cause, follow procedure on p. 84. If electric shock is the cause, move child from source of electricity (see p. 109).

Supplies: none.

Get professional help if:
• A child's heartbeat or breathing stops. Follow the steps below while waiting for emergency help.

AIRWAY:

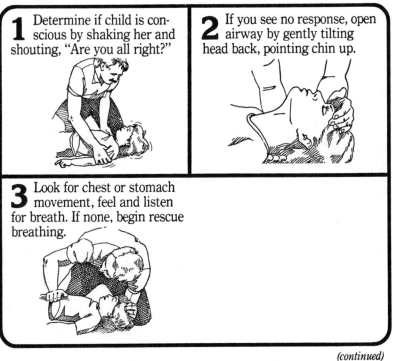

1 Determine if child is conscious by shaking her and shouting, "Are you all right?"

2 If you see no response, open airway by gently tilting head back, pointing chin up.

3 Look for chest or stomach movement, feel and listen for breath. If none, begin rescue breathing.

(continued)

CARDIAC ARREST (continued)

BREATHING:

1 *For an infant or child up to age 8,* cover mouth and nose with your mouth to administer breathing.

2 *For a child aged 8 or older,* cover only the mouth and pinch the nose closed.

3A *For an infant under 1 year,* give 4 quick puffs, and then 1 puff every 4 seconds.

3B *For a child aged 1 to 8,* give 4 quick breaths, and then 1 breath every 4 seconds.

3C *For a child aged 8 or older,* give 4 quick breaths, and then 1 breath every 5 seconds.

(continued)

CIRCULATION:

1 Check pulse: the carotid artery on the child's neck, and just above the left nipple on an infant.

2A *For infants,* use only the tips of the index and middle fingers to compress sternum 1/2-3/4 inches 80 to 100 times per minute.

2B *For children 1 to 8,* use heel of only one hand to compress at mid-sternum 3/4-1 1/2 inches 80 to 100 times per minute.

2C *For children older than 8,* kneel at the side and place the heel of one hand 1 1/2-2 inches above the lowest notch of the sternum; place the other hand on top and interlock fingers. With shoulders directly over sternum, compress chest 1-1 1/2 inches, release, but leave the heal of your hand touching the chest. Repeat, with an even period of compression and release. With solo resuscitation, give 15 compressions for every 2 quick breaths. Give 80 compressions per minute, stopping when giving breaths. With 2 people, give 60 compressions per minute.

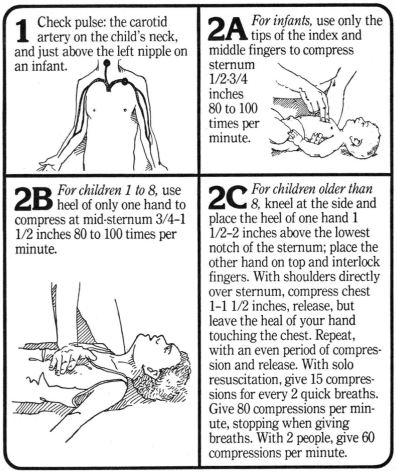

Related topics: Breathing Emergency, Drowning, Electric Shock.

CHEST PAIN

Description: discomfort in the chest associated with illnesses such as colds, flu, asthma.

What you need to know:
• Children commonly experience chest pain and, unlike in adults, it almost never indicates heart problems.
• Usually, it is harmless.
• The source of pain often is muscles made sore by coughing; another common cause is overexertion.

Get professional help if:
• Along with chest pain, your child has a high fever,* coughs blood, or has other symptoms of illness.
• A child repeatedly complains of pain under the armpits.
• The pain results from injury.
• Sudden chest pain occurs during an attack of asthma.

Supplies: thermometer, aspirin (ASA)/acetaminophen (acet.), heating pad or hot water bottle.

Symptoms:
• stabbing sensation related or not to breathing, laughing, coughing
• tightness or soreness in chest

What to check:
• Did pain begin suddenly or come on gradually? Where in the chest is it located?
• Is pain made worse by moving a particular part of the body?

Treatment:
• Give ASA/acet.
• Apply mild heat to sore muscles.
• If pain is from coughing, give cough medicine.

Related topics: Asthma, Bronchiolitis, Bronchitis, Cold, Hyperventilation.

*See Fever Guide, p. 27.

CHICKEN POX

Description: highly contagious virus marked by itching rash of blisters.

What you need to know:
- One attack of this common childhood disease gives immunity.
- It is contagious from 1 day before rash appears until blisters dry (about 7 days).
- Aspirin given to children with chicken pox has been linked to Reye's syndrome (p. 173).

Get professional help if:
- Rash shows signs of infection (redness, pus).
- Fever* persists after scabs begin to form.
- Lymph glands become enlarged and tender.
- High fever, headache, vomiting, disorientation or convulsions occur.

Supplies: thermometer, acetaminophen (acet.)—not aspirin (ASA), calamine lotion, fingernail scissors, gloves, baking soda or cornstarch (1/2 c./tub water), salt water (1 tsp./8-oz. glass water).

Symptoms:
- mild fever*
- fatigue/headache
- rash that progresses from red spots to blisters, which dry and form scabs
- itchy rash appears in "crops" over several days, so is present in different stages simultaneously.

What to check:
- Inspect the rash daily. It may spread to the mouth or vagina, but most will be on the face and trunk.
- Monitor temperature daily. It generally increases as blisters are forming and decreases as they dry; it's typically low-grade.

Treatment:
- Give acet. (not ASA) for itching, fever. Apply calamine lotion.
- Keep your child cool and quiet; minimize exposure to other children.
- Encourage him not to scratch; it may introduce infection or leave scars, especially on his face. Cut his fingernails or use gloves to reduce damage from scratching.
- Give cool or tepid baths in soda or cornstarch daily.
- Use saltwater gargle to soothe itching in mouth. (Note: discontinue use if gargling causes pain)

Related topics: Blister, Breathing Emergency, Impetigo, Poison Ivy, Reye's Syndrome, Shingles.

CHOKING

Description: a life-threatening obstruction of the airway by an object, food or croup.

What you need to know:	**Get professional help if:**
• The signals of choking: bluish lips, nails and skin; inability to speak, breathe or cry; high-pitched noises; ineffective coughs. • If breathing has stopped, *don't* begin emergency breathing until the airway is cleared.	• Choking lasts more than a minute. Have someone call the rescue squad while you begin emergency procedures. • Do *not* interfere with your child or call for help if she can still speak, cough or breathe.

Supplies: none.

1A *For a conscious infant:* Straddle her over your arm, face down with her upper chest and jaw in your hand. Give 4 quick blows between her shoulder blades with the heel of your hand.

1B Quickly turn her up on your other arm, resting it on your leg. With her head lower than her body, give 4 quick chest thrusts with 2 or 3 fingers. Repeat 1A and 1B until the object is dislodged or she loses consciousness.

2A *For an unconscious infant:* Attempt to restore breathing (see pp. 71–72 for details). Call for emergency help while continuing with 2B.

2B Try to locate and remove object from the airway. If object is removed and baby does not begin breathing, resume emergency breathing. Continue until help arrives or breathing starts.

(continued)

3A *For a conscious child:* Kneel and drape the child over your thighs with her head lower than her body. Give 4 blows to her back between her shoulder blades.

3B Gently turn her onto the floor and give 4 chest compressions (see pp. 71–72). Repeat 3A and 3B until object is dislodged or the child loses consciousness.

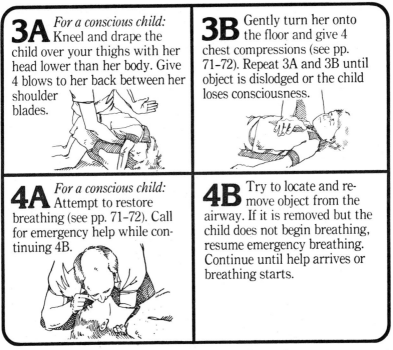

4A *For a conscious child:* Attempt to restore breathing (see pp. 71–72). Call for emergency help while continuing 4B.

4B Try to locate and remove object from the airway. If it is removed but the child does not begin breathing, resume emergency breathing. Continue until help arrives or breathing starts.

Related topics: Breathing Emergency, Cardiac Arrest, Croup.

COLD

Description: a highly contagious viral infection of nasal and throat membranes; frequently involves ears and chest.

What you need to know:
- Preschoolers have 5–8 colds a year; each cold lasts 7–10 days.
- Colds are most contagious in the first 3–4 days; symptoms usually subside after the third day. Ear infections are a common complication.
- Antibiotics don't cure colds and may worsen them or upset a child's stomach.

Get professional help if:
- Earache, sinus pain or chest pain develop.
- A child younger than 6 years old coughs up green or grey sputum.
- There are white or yellow spots on tonsils, throat.
- Cold symptoms and fever over 101°F. don't improve in 4 days*.

Supplies: thermometer, spoon handle as tongue depressor, penlight, liquids, nasal aspirator, salt water gargle, aspirin (ASA)/acetaminophen (acet.), throat lozenges.

Symptoms:
- congestion/runny nose
- postnasal drip/sore throat
- red, watery eyes
- neck, head, muscle aches
- sneezing
- dry cough/hoarseness
- breathing difficulty
- listlessness/loss of appetite
- fever*

What to check:
- Check temperature 3 times a day.
- Look down throat and record findings.

Treatment:
- Offer water or juice every hour. With infants, draw mucus from nose with a nasal aspirator before feedings and naps.
- Place infant on his side for sleeping; slightly elevate older children's heads.

- Have him gargle with salt water every 2 hours if he's 10 years old or older.
- Give ASA/acet. for fever.
- Give throat lozenges for sore throat to child age 5 or older.

Related topics: Allergy, Bronchiolitis, Bronchitis, Cough, Croup, Earache, Hay Fever, Headache, Laryngitis, Sinusitis, Sore Muscle, Strep Throat.

*See Fever Guide, p. 27.

COLD SORE/FEVER BLISTER

Description: sores in or around the mouth that are caused by herpes simplex virus.

What you need to know:
- It is a common condition for which there is no cure or vaccine.
- Sores may be inside or outside mouth on gums, tongue, lips, cheeks, throat.
- Sores may appear with colds and other infections, stress, fatigue.

Get professional help if:
- There are large, white patches on roof of mouth.
- Bad breath or spots on hands and feet appear with the blisters.
- Sores are so painful your child does not eat or drink, or aspirin or acetaminophen are not effective.
- Sores are in eyes.

Supplies: thermometer; cool, soft foods and drinks; straws; aspirin (ASA)/acetaminophen (acet.); topical anesthetic; cool compresses.

Symptoms:
- mouth sores that start as blisters and change to shallow ulcers
- fever*
- some cases may be so mild that there are no symptoms

What to check:
- Along with sores, are there symptoms of other conditions noted below?

Treatment:
- There is no home treatment except to relieve discomfort. Check with your doctor about possible new treatments.
- Give cool, soft foods and drinks to soothe mouth. Older children may use straws to bypass sores.
- Give ASA/acet. to relieve fever.
- Apply a topical oral anesthetic such as Xylocaine to sores inside mouth if your doctor recommends it.
- Cool compresses may help remove sores when they form crusts.

Related topics: Chicken Pox; Hand, Foot and Mouth Disease.

*See Fever Guide, p. 27.

COLIC

Description: prolonged periods of intense crying in infants, occurring repeatedly over several days, with no apparent cause.

What you need to know:
- It is very common in babies between ages 2–4 weeks and 3 months.
- It can be very frustrating to parents because there seems to be no reason for the crying, yet it may continue for hours.
- Get help early in the course of the problem.

Get professional help if:
- Your baby cries for more than 4 hours.
- There is fever,* runny nose, cough, vomiting, or other signs of illness.
- Colic is not subsiding by age 4 months.

Supplies: thermometer, pacifier, hot water bottle or heating pad.

Symptoms:
- spells usually occur in late afternoon, evening or in the night, often after feeding
- baby may act hungry, but begin crying part-way through feeding.
- legs may be drawn up to body and fists clenched

What to check:
- Possible causes of discomfort, such as illness, diaper pin, diaper rash, or hard pellet-like stools.
- If bottle-feeding, was formula prepared and administered properly, and does the formula flow from the upended bottle at one drop per second?

Treatment:
- It may be necessary to try a number of methods to soothe your baby; there is no sure-fire treatment and it is possible no method will have results. Be patient and wait it out. Try:
  –cuddling, soothing talk or music, rocking, walking, back-rub, pacifier
  –placing your baby on her stomach
  –burping your baby
  –applying heat to the baby's abdomen.
- Get some rest from caring for the infant, even if only for a few hours.
- Discuss your frustration with others.

Related topics: Constipation, Stomach Pain.

*See Fever Guide, p. 27.

CONCUSSION

Description: a blow to the head that can cause minor swelling, unconsciousness and/or amnesia.

What you need to know:
• Head blows are common and rarely a cause for concern.
• Serious injuries may cause internal bleeding which puts pressure on the brain.
• A good rule: the child is well if he or she acts well.

Get professional help if:
• Child loses consciousness (see p. 211).
• Child vomits more than twice.
• One pupil becomes larger than the other.
• Child behaves abnormally: slurred speech, double vision, loss of coordination.

Supplies: ice.

Symptoms:
• symptoms vary according to severity and location of the injury
• minor scalp bleeding and a "goose egg" are common after a bump
• odd behavior or loss of alertness indicate a more serious injury

What to check:
• How does the child act? If the injury is serious it will produce a symptom.
• Watch child closely for at least 6 hours after the injury, even if that requires waking a sleeping child every 2 hours.

Treatment:
• Watch child for signs of serious injury.
• Apply ice to injured area to relieve pain and reduce swelling.
• Treat blows that cause bleeding with ice and pressure. Head cuts bleed easily.

Related topics: Bruise, Cut/Wound.

CONSTIPATION

Description: hard bowel movements.

What you need to know:
• Most often caused by diet, illness or psychological factors, more rarely by congenital defect of the large intestine.
• Children differ greatly in their bowel habits; constipation refers to stool consistency only.

Get professional help if:
• Movements are painful.
• Stools are bloody.
• A toilet-trained child has soiled underwear.
• Child passes infrequent, but very large stools.
• Constipation recurs frequently.
• The condition does not improve with home treatment.

Supplies: foods such as fruit (except bananas), fruit juice, raw vegetables, grains; lots of water; unrefined sugars; Maltsupex.

Symptoms:
• hard stools
• painful bowel movements

What to check:
• Soiling of underwear may indicate that loose stools are leaking from plugged bowels.
• Is your child holding back BMs due to overemphasis of toilet training or to avoid pain?

Treatment:
• Consult your doctor by phone before giving such home remedies as laxatives, enemas, suppositories, mineral oil.
• Adjust the diet to include more roughage and fiber and fewer dairy products daily.
• *Do not* make the child anxious by treating the condition as a problem—downplay it.
• For an infant, add one teaspoon of Maltsupex to a bottle twice a day.

Related topics: Stomach Pain.

CONVULSION (FIT, SEIZURE)

Description: involuntary muscle spasms sometimes associated with periods of temporary unconsciousness, confusion.

What you need to know:
- A seizure is not life-threatening. Most seizures result from fever* (especially to age 3, rarely after age 6). Fever-related seizures usually end within 5 minutes and have no lasting effects.
- Other less common causes include poisoning, severe infection, epilepsy.

Get professional help if:
- It is your child's first seizure. Call a rescue squad if you need help transporting your child.
- A seizure lasts more than 10 minutes.

Supplies: thermometer, cool water and washcloth, aspirin (ASA) suppository.

Symptoms:
- blue face and lips
- uncontrolled, jerking body movements/rigidity
- loss of bladder and bowel control
- nausea/vomiting/drooling
- heart palpitations
- headache/stiff neck
- unconsciousness

What to check:
- How does your child act before and after convulsions?
- How long did the seizure last?
- Did it affect one or both sides of the body?
- Is there fever, or are symptoms present of infection, poisoning?

Treatment:
- Remove nearby objects the child may injure himself on; restrain gently. Loosen tight clothing.
- Make sure his airway is open; give emergency breathing if breathing stops (pp. 71-72).
- Turn him on side to prevent choking on vomit or saliva.

Don't place fingers, liquids, medication, etc. in his mouth.
- Wipe his body with cool washcloth. Don't place in bathtub. Give ASA suppository if fever is high.

Related topics: Breath-holding, Encephalitis, Meningitis.

*See Fever Guide, p. 27.

COUGH

Description: a reflexive spasm in response to an irritation of the respiratory system.

What you need to know:	Get professional help if:
• It can be caused by a variety of conditions, including virus, bacterial infection, asthma, allergy. • Coughing helps clear the respiratory system of irritants.	• Your child who is younger than 3 months old has a persistent cough. • Breathing is rapid, difficult or wheezy. • Fever* is persistent. • A cough lasts more than 10 days. • A foreign object has been swallowed.

Supplies: thermometer; liquids, such as water and fruit juices; cool mist vaporizer (optional); OTC cough medicine (optional).

Symptoms:	What to check:
• Coughing itself is a symptom of some other condition.	• Try to identify the cause of the cough to decide what treatment to use. • Check your child's temperature every 4–6 hours.

Treatment:	
• Treatment will depend on the type of cough (see related topics). • Give plenty of liquids to soothe the throat and loosen mucus. • Vaporizers may soothe irritation with croup and bronchitis.	• In general, use medicine only if coughing is interfering with sleep or making your child tired. (Consult your physician about what medication you should give.)

Related topics: Allergy, Asthma, Bronchitis, Choking, Cold, Croup, Sore Throat, Whooping Cough.

*See Fever Guide, p. 27.

CRADLE CAP (SEBORRHEA)

Description: a harmless skin condition characterized by oily, yellowish scales or crusted patches.

What you need to know:
• It is most common in infants, but occurs to age 6.
• Usually it is on the scalp, but may be on the forehead, eyebrows, behind ears or in the groin area.
• It is often a recurring condition.

Get professional help if:
• The condition persists after several weeks of home treatment.

Supplies: washcloth, soap and water, fine-tooth comb, antidandruff shampoo, baby oil, towel.

Symptoms:
• oily, yellowish scales
• crusting patches of skin with slight redness in surrounding areas

What to check:
• If an antidandruff shampoo causes scalp irritation, discontinue its use; take care to avoid the eyes.
• Watch for signs of skin infection—children with cradle cap are susceptible.

Treatment:
• Wash the affected area daily with soap and water, using a washcloth.
• Remove scales with a fine-tooth comb.
• If scales are on the scalp, and washing doesn't improve the condition, use antidandruff shampoo for children (not infants).
• With severe cases in infants and children, rub baby oil into the affected area and cover with a warm towel for 15 minutes. Then work scales loose with a comb and wash away.

Related topics: Eczema, Impetigo, Ringworm.

CREEPING ERUPTION

Description: penetration of skin by hookworm larvae (also termed *cutaneous larvae migrans*).

What you need to know:
- The larvae usually are contracted from sand or dirt in which infected dogs and cats have defecated.
- It can be anywhere on the body, but is most common on feet, hands, buttocks.

Get professional help if:
- Symptoms are present. The condition is easily treated, but requires oral medicine that must be prescribed by a doctor.

Supplies: prescribed antiworm medication (often thiabendazole).

Symptoms:
- wavy, red lines on the skin (the width of a pencil and several inches long)
- itchy skin rash

What to check:
- Is the child's play area contaminated by dog and cat feces? If so, have your child wear shoes.

Treatment:
- Administer medication prescribed by your doctor.
- Consult a veterinarian about decontaminating play areas.
- Take measures to prevent contamination:

–have pets checked regularly for hookworm.
–cover your child's sandbox when it is not being used.

Related topics: Blood Poisoning, Impetigo, Scabies.

CROSSED EYES

Description: inward or outward turning of one or both eyes rather than parallel eye motion.

What you need to know:
• Periodic crossing of the eyes is normal in infants until they develop eye coordination (3–6 months).
• Crossing may result from an imbalance in eye muscles or a visual defect such as near- or far-sightedness.

Get professional help if:
• Symptoms are present. If there is doubt, see an ophthalmologist. The condition must be treated to prevent permanent damage.

Supplies: none.

Symptoms:
• one or both eyes appear to be crossed most or all of the time beyond age 4–6 months (eyes don't "track")

What to check:
• Don't be fooled: the small amount of white in a baby's eyes may create the illusion that they are crossed, especially when she is looking to one side.

Treatment:
• There are no home remedies. If you suspect crossed eyes, have your child examined by an ophthalmologist (even before age 6 months).
• Doctor's treatment may involve wearing a patch over the "lazy" eye, glasses, exercises to strengthen the eye muscles, surgery.

Related topics: Vision Problem.

CROUP

Description: a barking cough or labored breathing caused by inflammation and constriction of airways.

What you need to know:
- An attack often comes on suddenly (usually at night), for no apparent reason. It requires immediate home treatment.
- Children under age 3 are most susceptible because their air passages are small.
- It is caused by a virus.

Get professional help if:
- Symptoms worsen rapidly and home treatment doesn't ease the condition in 30–40 minutes.
- Fever is above 103°F.*
- Child turns blue or drools.

Supplies: thermometer, vaporizer, aspirin (ASA)/acetaminophen (acet.), liquids.

Symptoms:
- a hacking cough that sounds like the bark of a seal or dog
- difficulty breathing air *into* the lungs
- fever*
- hoarseness

What to check:
- Don't leave your child unattended during an attack.
- Since an attack may occur several nights in a row, watch the child closely for 3 nights; you may sleep in the same room if it is convenient.

Treatment:
- While most cases can be treated at home, contact your doctor at the onset of an attack.
- Take your child into the bathroom, close door, run hot water to generate steam.
- If condition doesn't improve in 20 minutes, take her into the cool night air for 20 minutes. If still no improvement, seek help immediately.
- If the doctor determines home treatment is sufficient, put a vaporizer in the room, give ASA/acet. and liquids.
- *Don't* give cough syrup.

Related topics: Allergy, Asthma, Breathing Emergency, Bronchitis, Choking, Cough, Diphtheria, Laryngitis, Whooping Cough.

*See Fever Guide, p. 27.

CUT/WOUND

Description: any break in skin, such as an abrasion, laceration, puncture, cut or scrape.

What you need to know:
• Panic and fear increase heart rate and speed blood loss, so keep your child calm.
• Over half of all cuts/wounds can be handled safely at home without professional help.

Get professional help if:
• Wound is deep or longer than 1 inch, pain persists over 12 hours, or edges of cut separate.
• Bleeding persists after 15 minutes of pressure.
• Last tetanus shot was 10 years ago or longer.
• Wound is dirty or infected.

Supplies: clean cloth, ice in plastic bag, soap and water or 3% hydrogen peroxide solution, antibacterial ointment (like Bacitracin), gauze, tape, thermometer.

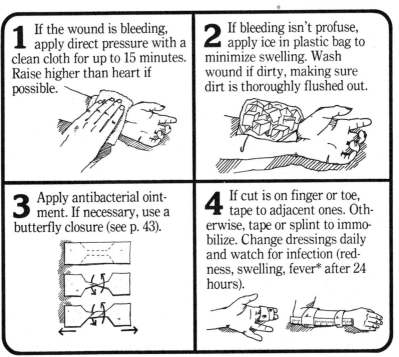

1 If the wound is bleeding, apply direct pressure with a clean cloth for up to 15 minutes. Raise higher than heart if possible.

2 If bleeding isn't profuse, apply ice in plastic bag to minimize swelling. Wash wound if dirty, making sure dirt is thoroughly flushed out.

3 Apply antibacterial ointment. If necessary, use a butterfly closure (see p. 43).

4 If cut is on finger or toe, tape to adjacent ones. Otherwise, tape or splint to immobilize. Change dressings daily and watch for infection (redness, swelling, fever* after 24 hours).

Related topics: Blood Poisoning, Eye Injury, Severed Limb, Tetanus.

*See Fever Guide, p. 27.

CYSTIC FIBROSIS

Description: a hereditary disease that affects the mucus-producing glands in the lungs and intestines.

What you need to know:
• Digestive problems result from blockage of the intestines and lack of certain enzymes in the pancreas.
• Respiratory problems result from blockage of airways with mucus and from infection.

Get professional help if:
• Symptoms are present. There is no cure for cystic fibrosis. Early detection will reduce permanent lung damage. Treatment is essential to prolong life.

Supplies: prescribed medication, including special diet, vitamin supplements; cool mist vaporizer.

Symptoms:
• chronic cough
• labored breathing
• fatigue
• diarrhea or constipation with foul-smelling stools
• failure to gain weight
• salty sweat
• protruding rectum

What to check:
• Watch for symptoms of respiratory infections.
• If there is a history of cystic fibrosis in your family, have your child checked by a doctor.

Treatment:
• It must be prescribed by a doctor and followed carefully. It may include:
–prescribed medications
–physical therapy to loosen and drain mucus from the lungs
–special diet
–vitamin supplements
–exposure to moist air

Related topics: Asthma, Breathing Emergency, Bronchiolitis, Bronchitis, Constipation, Diarrhea, Pneumonia.

DEHYDRATION

Description: a condition in which there is an insufficient amount of fluid in the body.

What you need to know:
- The most common causes are diarrhea and vomiting.
- Other causes are excessive sweating and urination.
- Body fluids contain important salts and minerals that must be replaced when the child is dehydrated.

Get professional help if:
- Symptoms are severe.
- Your child is not able to keep down liquids due to vomiting or diarrhea.
- Home remedies don't improve the condition.
- Your child has diabetes and shows signs of dehydration.

Supplies: thermometer; liquids, including carbonated drinks, commercial mixes (such as Lytren, Pedialyte), fruit juice, whole or skim milk diluted with equal parts of water.

Symptoms:
- dry mouth
- sunken eyes
- drowsiness
- lack of energy
- doughy-textured skin
- decreased urine output
- fever*

What to check:
- Is your child urinating infrequently? (Young children should not go more than 8 hours without urinating, older children 12 hours.) If so, increase liquid consumption.

Treatment:
- Give small amounts of cool liquids at least every hour if cause is vomiting (allow 2 hours after the last spell of vomiting). Recommended amounts for children of different ages during a 6-hour period are:

–infants—12 oz.
–preschool—24 oz.
–school-age—30 oz.

Related topics: Diabetes, Diarrhea, Heat Exhaustion, Heat Stroke, Vomiting.

*See Fever Guide, p. 27.

DIABETES

Description: an accumulation of sugar in the blood due to a lack of insulin in the body.

What you need to know:
- Insulin is a hormone made in the pancreas; it permits sugar to pass from the blood to cells.
- A lack of insulin causes sugar to collect in the blood and the cells to be deprived of sugar.
- A family history of diabetes is often present.

Get professional help if:
- You see symptoms of diabetes. (They may appear suddenly in children.)

Supplies: equipment to test urine or blood and administer insulin, prescribed medication (insulin, glucagon), proper diet.

Symptoms:
- frequent and increased urination (possibly bedwetting)
- thirst/increased appetite
- weight loss/fatigue
- irritability
- rapid, deep breathing
- dehydration/coma
- strange odor to the breath

What to check:
- After a professional diagnosis, watch for reaction to too much insulin (see hypoglycemia).
- Also watch for infections, colds, stomach flu, which may change the insulin requirement.

Treatment:
- A doctor will prescribe a program of treatment that must be closely followed at home on a daily basis. It usually includes:
-testing of the sugar level in urine or blood
-insulin injections to lower blood sugar level
-glucagon injections to raise blood sugar level if there is an insulin reaction
-carefully monitored diet.

Related topics: Bedwetting, Dehydration, Hypoglycemia, Urinary Tract Infection.

DIAPER RASH

Description: a rash on a baby's bottom in the areas covered by a diaper.

What you need to know:
- Diaper rashes are caused by diapers. The simplest cure is letting your baby go bare-bottomed.
- Rubber pants can aggravate the rash.
- Most babies get diaper rash.

Get professional help if:
- The rash starts looking angry or the rash pimples develop whiteheads or blisters.
- Home treatment fails to improve the rash in a few days.

Supplies: water, baby ointment with zinc oxide.

Symptoms:
- red patches, with tiny pimples, on skin areas covered by the diaper

What to check:
- Is the baby allergic to some substance that comes in contact with the red area? Possibilities include rubber pants, detergents, powders, lanolin, perfumes, alcohol, lotions, fabric softeners, etc.

Treatment:
- Increase the frequency of diaper changes, cleaning your baby carefully each time with plain water.
- Apply zinc oxide ointment between skin and diaper.
- Let the baby go diaperless as much as possible.

DIARRHEA

Description: frequent liquid or soft bowel movements (BMs) that are light brown or green in color.

What you need to know:
- Causes include virus, bacteria, parasites, diet change, antibiotics, intolerance to milk.
- Often it is present with colds, sore throat or infections of the stomach and intestines.
- Diarrhea *alone* rarely leads to dehydration.

Get professional help if:
- Loose BMs occur more than once an hour for more than 12 hours.
- There is fever of 102.5°F. for more than 4 hours.*
- Abdominal pain is present for more than 1/2 hour.
- Blood is present in stools.

Supplies: thermometer, clear liquids (juice, soda, Gatorade), selected foods, petroleum jelly.

Symptoms:
- liquid or soft bowel movements
- BMs increase in frequency to more than 2 a day
- abdominal cramps prior to BMs

What to check:
- Are there signs of dehydration (see p. 99)?
- Is your child passing urine normally?
- How frequent are BMs and what is their consistency?
- If an infant, has his diet changed recently? Check temperature.

Treatment:
- If there are 4 stools a day or less, don't change diet, but confine eating to mealtimes.
- For more severe diarrhea, rest intestinal tract by stopping milk, solid foods for 24 hours.
- During this time, provide clear liquids (water, apple juice, soda pop). Do not push liquids, merely make them available.
- After 24 hours off food, begin feeding with fruit, crackers, toast, cereal.
- On the third day, return to the normal diet.
- Put petroleum jelly on the buttocks or around the diaper area if it is sore.

Related topics: Cystic Fibrosis, Dehydration, Diaper Rash, Stomach Flu, Stomach Pain, Vomiting.

*See Fever Guide, p. 27.

DIPHTHERIA

Description: a contagious bacterial infection that affects the respiratory system, nerves, muscles, heart.

What you need to know:
- Vaccine gives immunity. *Get your child immunized.*
- Once fully immunized, a person will not contract diphtheria but may carry it.
- Untreated, it often results in death.
- It is easily confused with strep throat, mononucleosis, croup.

Get professional help if:
- Your child is unimmunized. See your doctor when your child is 2 months old to begin the immunization program.

Supplies: thermometer, antibiotics, other drugs.

Symptoms:
- sore, white throat and tonsils
- fever*/headache
- runny nose
- hoarseness/croup-like cough
- pneumonia/heart failure/paralyzed muscles

What to check:
- Has your child been properly immunized? Three shots should be given at 2-month intervals in infancy. Boosters should be given at 18 months of age, at school-age, and every 10 years thereafter.

Treatment:
- There is no home treatment. A doctor may prescribe antibiotics and other drugs to combat the infection. Severe cases may require a tracheotomy.
- Diphtheria is a serious condition that calls for prompt professional treatment. It usually occurs among unimmunized adults.

Related topics: Sore Throat, Tonsilitis.

*See Fever Guide, p. 27.

DIZZINESS

Description: an unsteady or whirling sensation associated with various conditions.

What you need to know:
- Dizziness often occurs with ear infections, strep throat, sinus infections, anemia, head injuries, and rarely, brain tumors.
- It is often accompanied by such symptoms as headache, fever,* nausea, earache.

Get professional help if:
- Dizziness occurs for more than 24 hours.
- There is a loss of coordination, earache, nausea, vomiting, unsteadiness, loss of consciousness.
- Dizziness occurs during or right after strenuous activity.

Supplies: thermometer.

Symptoms:
- loss of balance
- lack of coordination
- nausea
- vomiting

What to check:
- How long does the sensation of dizziness last?
- Are there other symptoms that may help explain the cause of dizziness?
- If your child says he's "dizzy," be sure he means dizzy, not nauseated or lightheaded.

Treatment:
- Dizziness itself does not generally require treatment; rather, it is a symptom of some other condition and will disappear as that condition is treated.
- For immediate relief, have your child lie down or sit bent over.
- Keep him quiet until feelings of dizziness disappear.

Related topics: Breath-holding, Ear Infection, Fainting, Hyperventilation, Unconsciousness.

*See Fever Guide, p. 27.

DROWNING

Description: suffocation by liquid, usually water.

What you need to know:
• Don't enter the water to rescue a child who can be reached with your arm, a boat, an extended object, or a throwable object.
• Give artificial respiration even to children who have been submerged a long time.

Get professional help if:
• The child has inhaled water into her lungs. After you are sure the child is breathing, treat for shock (see p. 184) and seek medical assistance immediately.

Supplies: towel, fishing pole, rope or other object that can be extended; buoyant object that can be thrown, such as board, life ring.

1 If the child is near the edge of water, kneel or lie down and reach out with your arm, towel or other object. Grab her wrist and pull her to shore.

2 If the child is beyond reach, wade into the water and see if an object can be extended to her. If she's in deep water, swim out (only if you are a competent swimmer); or use a boat, throw a floatable object, or call for help.

3 If possible, have the child hold onto the boat or extended object while you return to shore. If she's unconscious, begin artificial respiration while still in the water.

4 When on land, give emergency breathing if needed, *even if the child has been under water a long time* (see pp. 71–72). Treat for shock (see p. 184) and seek medical assistance. Keep the child warm.

Related topics: Breathing Emergency, Cardiac Arrest, Unconsciousness.

EARACHE

Description: an inflammation or accumulation of fluid in the middle ear, usually caused by bacterial infection.

What you need to know:
- Earaches are common in children under age 6.
- Colds often cause Eustachian tubes to swell and close. Fluids build up in the middle ear, causing pain and temporary hearing loss.

Get professional help if:
- Your child complains of ear pain or tugs, rubs ear(s).
- Dizziness or loss of hearing develops.
- Temperature is over 102°F.*
- Eardrum ruptures. Look for yellow to brown fluid draining from ear.

Supplies: thermometer, aspirin (ASA)/acetaminophen (acet.), prescribed eardrops, heating pad or hot water bottle.

Symptoms:
- aching/pain/sound in ear
- chills/fever*
- congestion, runny nose
- dizziness/headache
- ear discharge
- fussing/irritability
- inability to sleep
- hearing loss
- rubbing/tugging at ear

What to check:
- Monitor fever.

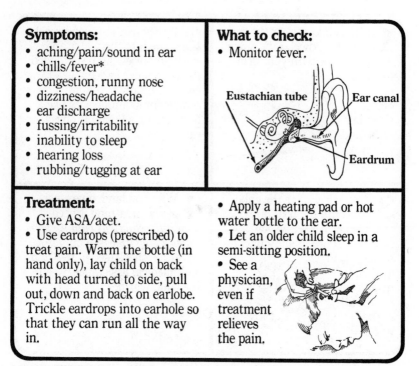

Eustachian tube   Ear canal

Eardrum

Treatment:
- Give ASA/acet.
- Use eardrops (prescribed) to treat pain. Warm the bottle (in hand only), lay child on back with head turned to side, pull out, down and back on earlobe. Trickle eardrops into earhole so that they can run all the way in.
- Apply a heating pad or hot water bottle to the ear.
- Let an older child sleep in a semi-sitting position.
- See a physician, even if treatment relieves the pain.

Related topics: Cold, Dizziness, Hearing Loss, Swimmer's Ear.

*See Fever Guide, p. 27.

EAR INJURY

Description: a severe cut or perforation of the eardrum resulting from a blow or other trauma.

What you need to know:	**Get professional help if:**
• Never insert an instrument in the ear to remove a foreign object. • If an ear is severed, pack it in ice and go immediately to medical help. • Don't let your child hit herself on the side of the head to restore hearing.	• Blood is flowing from ear. • White or yellow discharge from ear is seen. See your doctor within 6 hours. • Hearing is impaired after the injury.

Supplies: cottonballs, gauze or cloth patch, gauze strip.

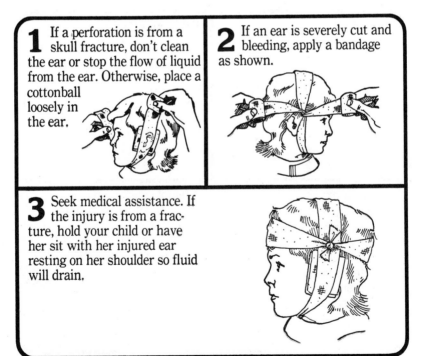

1 If a perforation is from a skull fracture, don't clean the ear or stop the flow of liquid from the ear. Otherwise, place a cottonball loosely in the ear.

2 If an ear is severely cut and bleeding, apply a bandage as shown.

3 Seek medical assistance. If the injury is from a fracture, hold your child or have her sit with her injured ear resting on her shoulder so fluid will drain.

Related topics: Cut/Wound.

ECZEMA

Description: an inherited condition characterized by a dry, scaly skin rash and intense itching.

What you need to know:
- The cause is unknown. Outbreaks may be triggered by emotional upset, allergic reaction, dry winter heat.
- Many children with eczema develop hay fever, asthma, allergies later in life.
- Often disappears with use of proper lotions.

Get professional help if:
- Home treatment does not improve the condition within a week.
- The rash becomes infected.

Supplies: OTC or prescribed hydrocortisone ointment, superfatted soap (Basis, Lowila, Aveeno, Oilatum), vaporizer.

Symptoms:
- pink or red rash
- intense itching
- when scratched, rash oozes a moist substance that dries and aggravates itching

What to check:
- Was a new food, fiber or substance recently introduced to or put on your child?
- Is soap rinsed thoroughly from body after baths?
- Is he emotionally upset?
- Do relatives have eczema?

Treatment:
- Relieve itching with hydrocortisone ointment.
- Use superfatted soap and give baths infrequently.
- Keep air moist with a vaporizer.
- If a particular food is the cause, eliminate it from the child's diet. However, do *not* attempt extensive dietary changes without a doctor's supervision.
- Cut your child's fingernails short to reduce irritation from scratching.

Related topics: Allergy, Cradle Cap.

ELECTRIC SHOCK

Description: severely reduced blood pressure, unconsciousness or burns resulting from contact with electrical current.

What you need to know:

• Do not touch the child directly if she is still touching the source of electricity.
• Emergency breathing (see pp. 71–72) may be needed, *then* treatment for burns (see p. 77).
• The injury a baby sustains from biting on a cord is often more serious than it appears.

Get professional help if:

• Severe electric shock occurs. Have someone else call for help while you try to free the child from the source of electricity.
• Electrical burn occurs.
• Child isn't breathing.
• There is an injury on the mouth.

Supplies: dry rubber or cloth mat or stack of newspapers, dry wooden stick (broomstick, board, etc.).

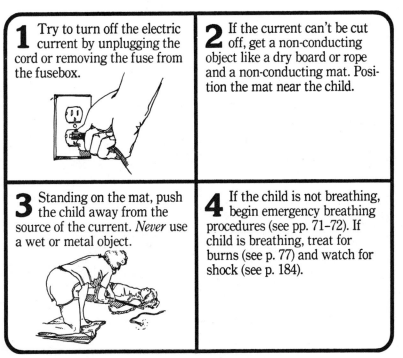

1 Try to turn off the electric current by unplugging the cord or removing the fuse from the fusebox.

2 If the current can't be cut off, get a non-conducting object like a dry board or rope and a non-conducting mat. Position the mat near the child.

3 Standing on the mat, push the child away from the source of the current. *Never* use a wet or metal object.

4 If the child is not breathing, begin emergency breathing procedures (see pp. 71–72). If child is breathing, treat for burns (see p. 77) and watch for shock (see p. 184).

Related topics: Breathing Emergency, Burn, Cardiac Arrest, Unconsciousness.

ENCEPHALITIS

Description: an inflammation of the brain; a rare but extremely serious condition.

What you need to know:
• The most common cause is infection by a virus.
• Other causes are bacterial infection, antitoxins introduced in vaccines, poisons (lead, mercury), bites of infected mosquitoes and parasites.

Get professional help if:
• Your child shows symptoms of encephalitis. It is a life-threatening condition that requires immediate attention.
• Your child has a severe reaction to any vaccine. Inform your doctor before a booster shot is given.

Supplies: thermometer.

Symptoms:
• stiffness and reduced mobility of the neck
• fever*
• headache
• vomiting
• sleepiness/confusion
• convulsions

What to check:
• Can your child bend his neck forward to touch his chest?
• Can he sit up without assistance?
• Be aware that, in rare cases, encephalitis develops as a complication of chicken pox, influenza, measles, mumps, rubella and other diseases.

Treatment:
• There is no home treatment.
• Treatment by a physician may involve tests to diagnose the condition and hospitalization.

Related topics: Headache, Vomiting.

*See Fever Guide, p. 27.

EPIGLOTTITIS

Description: a throat infection that constricts the airway and causes a croup-like difficulty in breathing.

What you need to know:
- Epiglottitis is a more serious condition than croup, which it resembles, and can constitute a medical emergency.
- Proper and prompt medical treatment is *always* necessary, and should cure the illness.

Get professional help if:
- You suspect the illness may be epiglottitis.
- Placing child in a humidified room fails to ease the breathing difficulty in 30 minutes. *Seek medical help immediately.*
- Your child's lips or skin appear bluish or she is drooling.

Supplies: cool mist vaporizer.

Symptoms:
- breathing difficulty, usually at night
- drooling
- child may sit with jaw pointed forward to open the throat passage
- symptoms persist even when the child is placed in a humidified room

What to check:
- Has the child swallowed some object that is interfering with breathing?
- Is the child hoarse? A child with croup *will* be, but one with epiglottitis *may not* be hoarse.

Treatment:
- Take your child into a room with a vaporizer or into a bathroom with a running shower or tub.
- *Keep your child calm.* Panic will contribute to the breathing difficulty.
- Keep car windows open enough to allow her to breathe cool night air (if weather permits) on the way to medical attention.

Related topics: Cough, Croup, Sore Throat.

EYE INJURY

Description: any of the following five basic types of injuries:
-1 Foreign objects (dust, dirt, gravel) in the eye
-2 Blows or scratches to the eye
-3 Burning of the eye with acid or alkali chemicals (battery acid, detergent, cleanser, etc.)
-4 Cuts of the eyeball or eyelid
-5 Objects impaled in the eye.

What you need to know:
• Prevent your child from rubbing an injured eye. Don't try to open your child's eye forcibly.
• Wash your hands before touching your child's eye.
• Eyes move together: if you need to restrict movement in one eye, you should bandage both.

Get professional help if:
• Your child's eye is injured or you cannot remove a foreign object yourself.
• Purple discoloration develops around eye within 3 hours after a blow. Black eyes that show a day after a blow are not a cause for alarm.

Supplies: tissue, cotton swab, water, bandage, cold compress, baking soda.

FOREIGN OBJECTS IN EYE:

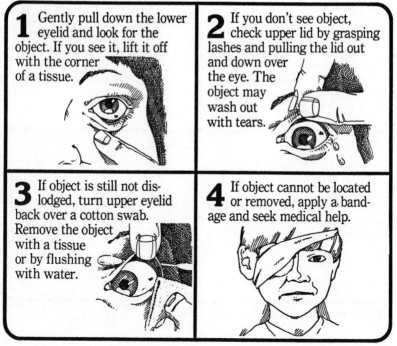

1 Gently pull down the lower eyelid and look for the object. If you see it, lift it off with the corner of a tissue.

2 If you don't see object, check upper lid by grasping lashes and pulling the lid out and down over the eye. The object may wash out with tears.

3 If object is still not dislodged, turn upper eyelid back over a cotton swab. Remove the object with a tissue or by flushing with water.

4 If object cannot be located or removed, apply a bandage and seek medical help.

(continued)

BLOWS AND SCRATCHES TO THE EYE:

1 Have your child lie down. If eye is bleeding, treat as described for cuts (see p. 97).

2 If eye is not bleeding, apply a sterile bandage. Treat as for a bruise (see p. 76).

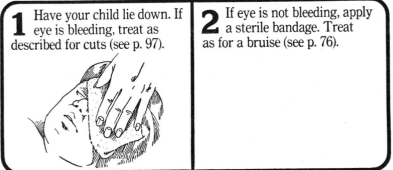

CHEMICAL BURNS OF THE EYE:

1 Begin flushing the eye with water *immediately*. Turn your child's head so the injured eye is down and cover the uninjured eye with your hand to keep the chemical out.

2 Continue flushing for 15 minutes with *water* for alkali burns (detergent, cleaning solution). If possible, flush with *soda* solution (1 teaspoon to a quart of water) for 10 minutes for acid burns.

3 When flushing, hold the eyelid open and pour water or solution in corner of eye so it flows to outer corner.

4 Don't attempt to remove chemical particles from the eye. Apply a loose bandage, keep your child from rubbing, and get medical help.

(continued)

113

CUTS OF THE EYE/EYELID:

1 If the *eyelid* is cut, apply direct pressure to stop bleeding. Clean the cut, place a sterile bandage over it and seek medical help immediately. Take along a cold compress to reduce bleeding, swelling and subsequent bruising.

2 If the *eyeball* is cut, do not apply pressure. Cover both eyes with a loose gauze or cloth bandage and seek medical help.

OBJECTS IMPALED IN THE EYE:

1 Don't wash eye or attempt to remove the object. Have your child lie on her back. Cover both eyes with a loose bandage. Restrain her hands if necessary.

2 Seek medical help immediately. Notify the doctor or hospital that you are coming. Keep your child lying down while en route.

Related topics: Bruise, Cut/Wound.

FEVER

Description: an oral temperature of over 100°F. or a rectal temperature of over 100.5°F.

What you need to know:
• Fever is usually a *symptom* of a viral or bacterial infection. It is not a disease. Normal body temperature ranges from 97–100°F. It varies according to time of day, activity level, age (infants', children's temperatures are higher than adults'); emotions; food consumption; and other factors.

Get professional help if:
• Your infant under 6 months has a fever. Your child has a fever over 104°F. without other symptoms, or lower fever without other symptoms that lasts over 24 hours. She has serious underlying illness and has any degree of fever. A seizure occurs or other symptoms suggest that you should call a doctor.

Supplies: thermometer, aspirin (ASA)/acetaminophen (acet.), liquids, tepid water, washcloth.

Symptoms:
• body warm to touch (not always reliable)
• rapid breathing
• flushed face
• increased need for sleep
• chills
• sweating
• glazed eyes

What to check:
• Does your child appear to be uncomfortable (losing sleep, not eating, fussy, listless)? If not, it may not be necessary to treat the fever.
• If fever is over 104°F., check temperature every 4 hours (unless she is asleep).

Treatment:
• See the Fever Guide, p. 27.
• Treatment is aimed at making the child more comfortable.
• Dress her in cool, cotton clothing (diapers, underwear, light pajamas).
• Give ASA/acet. according to recommended doses *and* timing on label (see p. 30).

• Offer liquids frequently.
• If the fever is over 104°F. an hour after dosing with ASA/acet., sponge her with tepid water. Continue sponging until fever drops.

FIFTH DISEASE

Description: a harmless but contagious rash that disappears on its own.

What you need to know:
• The rash usually appears first on the face, looking as if the child's cheeks had been slapped. A lacy rash may also appear on the trunk.
• It is common, harmless and self-curing.

Get professional help if:
• Your child has a rash and you believe it is caused by something more serious, such as scarlet fever or measles.

Supplies: thermometer.

Symptoms:
• red, lacy rash that begins on the face and spreads to back of arms and legs
• fading and intensifying of rash from hour to hour for about 10 days

What to check:
• Is there a fever* or any other symptom? If so, the rash is probably not fifth disease.

Treatment:
• There is no treatment and no need for treatment.
• It may recur for weeks, especially in response to skin irritation and temperature extremes. Still, no treatment is required.

*See Fever Guide, p. 27.

116

FINGERNAIL/TIP INJURY

Description: blow to fingertip causing intense pain, swelling, and black and blue fingernail.

What you need to know:
• Over 90% of fingertip injuries can be treated at home.
• When a fingertip receives a hard blow, the nail turns black and blue in several hours. Intense pain comes from accumulated blood trapped between nail and bone. Releasing the blood reduces the pain.

Get professional help if:
• Bone deformity suggests fracture or dislocation.
• Inability to straighten finger suggests damage to tendon.
• Drilling (shown below) is impossible — child is uncooperative or tip is badly swollen.
• Pain persists after drilling.

Supplies: ice or cold water, nail or paperclip, sharp blade or penknife, cloth or gauze, gauze bandage.

1 Apply ice or cold water as soon as possible to reduce swelling.

2 Heat a blade, nail or paperclip with a match. Hold the finger firmly in place and burn a hole through the nail.

3 When hole is through nail, place tip of gauze or cloth into hole to absorb blood. Pain should be relieved immediately.

4 Cover hole with a gauze bandage so blood continues to drain. Keep nail covered for a few days.

Related topics: Bruise, Cut/Wound.

FISH HOOK IN SKIN

Description: a fish hook embedded anywhere in the skin.

What you need to know:
• The barb at the point of the hook is what makes removal difficult; if you have small children, flatten barbs with. pliers.
• Novocaine or other local anesthetic shots may cause as much pain as removal of the hook.

Get professional help if:
• Your child's last tetanus shot was more than 5 years ago.
• The wound becomes infected.

Supplies: wire cutter, cord, water, hydrogen peroxide (3%), bandage.

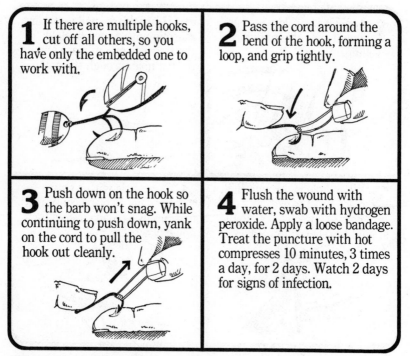

1 If there are multiple hooks, cut off all others, so you have only the embedded one to work with.

2 Pass the cord around the bend of the hook, forming a loop, and grip tightly.

3 Push down on the hook so the barb won't snag. While continuing to push down, yank on the cord to pull the hook out cleanly.

4 Flush the wound with water, swab with hydrogen peroxide. Apply a loose bandage. Treat the puncture with hot compresses 10 minutes, 3 times a day, for 2 days. Watch 2 days for signs of infection.

Related topics: Cut/Wound, Tetanus.

FROSTBITE

Description: freezing of skin tissue and fluid as a result of exposure to extreme cold.

What you need to know:

• Skin may become flushed, then turn glossy, grayish-yellow. Blisters may form.
• The most frequently injured areas are fingers, ears, nose, toes and cheeks.
• Victims may not be aware of their condition; they may also have hypothermia (see p. 142).

Get professional help if:

• Your child suffers from frostbite. Permanent damage can occur if frostbitten tissue is not handled properly. But thaw the affected parts *before* you travel to the doctor.

Supplies: warm water (102–105°F./ or feels warm on the elbow), sheets and blankets, warm fluids (hot chocolate, tea, soup—no alcoholic beverages), sterile cloth or gauze.

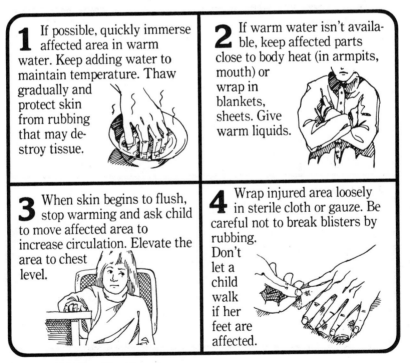

1 If possible, quickly immerse affected area in warm water. Keep adding water to maintain temperature. Thaw gradually and protect skin from rubbing that may destroy tissue.

2 If warm water isn't available, keep affected parts close to body heat (in armpits, mouth) or wrap in blankets, sheets. Give warm liquids.

3 When skin begins to flush, stop warming and ask child to move affected area to increase circulation. Elevate the area to chest level.

4 Wrap injured area loosely in sterile cloth or gauze. Be careful not to break blisters by rubbing. Don't let a child walk if her feet are affected.

Related topics: Hypothermia.

GEOGRAPHIC TONGUE

Description: a condition in which the tongue is marked with smooth patches, so that it resembles a map.

What you need to know:
- It is a common and harmless condition that requires no treatment.
- It is not painful and does not affect a child's ability to taste.

Get professional help if:
- You feel unsure of the diagnosis.

Supplies: none.

Symptoms:
- smooth patches of different colors, sizes and shapes on the tongue

What to check:
- The pattern may change slowly, disappearing and recurring over a period of years.

Treatment:
- There is no treatment and no need for treatment. Reassure your child that nothing is wrong with him.

GERMAN MEASLES (RUBELLA)

Description: a common, contagious viral disease with a characteristic rash.

What you need to know:
• Also called "3-day measles," rubella resembles 7-day measles but cold symptoms are absent or minor.
• a vaccine is available for children over age 15 months. *Get your child immunized.*
• It is relatively harmless to all but unborn children.

Get professional help if:
• A pregnant woman without immunity is exposed to it (first 3 months of pregnancy are the most risky). A vaccine can be given to protect the fetus from permanent injury (blindness, deafness, heart disease).

Supplies: thermometer, aspirin (ASA)/acetaminophen (acet.).

Symptoms:
• low fever* and mild runny nose followed by rash in 1–2 days
• swollen glands in back of neck, behind ears
• a rash of small, red, slightly raised spots
• joint pain and swelling

What to check:
• A case of rubella may be so mild that there are no detectable symptoms.
• Rashes usually begin on the face and spread to the rest of body in a day. They usually disappear in 3 days.

Treatment:
• A child is contagious 7 days before to 5 days after the rash appears; incubation takes 14–21 days.
• Give ASA/acet. for fever and pain.

Related topics: Arthritis, Swollen Lymph Gland.

*See Fever Guide, p. 27.

GOITER

Description: a lump or swelling in the neck, resulting from an enlarged thyroid gland.

What you need to know:
• Goiter is commonly caused by a deficiency of iodine, but has other possible causes.

Get professional help if:
• You suspect this condition affects your child; it must be diagnosed and treated by a physician.

Supplies: prescribed medication.

Symptoms:
• a lump in the midsection of the neck, usually below and at both sides of the Adam's apple; often it can be felt as well as seen.
• difficulty swallowing

What to check:
• Make sure you don't mistake swollen lymph glands for a goiter. They are much smaller, and don't appear in the center of the neck.

Treatment:
• There is no home remedy.
• A doctor's treatment may include oral prescription drugs and, in rare instances, surgery.

Related topics: Swollen Lymph Gland, Thyroid Problem.

GUM BOIL

Description: an abscess near a decaying or injured tooth, usually near a baby tooth.

What you need to know:
• If untreated, infection from a gum boil near a baby tooth may damage the permanent tooth that lies underneath it. Infection also may result in premature loss of baby teeth, causing long-term orthodontic problems.

Get professional help if:
• A gum boil is present—even if it is near a baby tooth that might naturally come out soon.

Supplies: aspirin (ASA)/acetaminophen (acet.), saltwater solution (pinch of salt in 1 c. water).

Symptoms:
• raised boil on gum that resembles a pimple; it eventually breaks and discharges pus
• tender gum near the abscess
• sometimes, bluish discoloration of the tooth

What to check:
• Has your child recently had a tooth filled? Gum boils often develop after a cavity is repaired.
• Has he suffered a mouth injury? If so, watch for signs of infection for 1-2 months.

Treatment:
• Don't rely on home treatment; *see a dentist.* The dentist's treatment may include removing the affected tooth; however, such drastic measures are not always necessary.
• If the boil is near a baby tooth, ease pain by giving ASA/acet. or, if the child is over age 3, by having her swish saltwater solution around in her mouth.
• Never put ASA directly on a child's gum to ease pain—it will burn gum tissue.

HAIR LOSS

Description: a temporary loss of hair when hair and scalp underneath are healthy.

What you need to know:
• In most cases, hair will regrow naturally in 12 months. However, a similar hair loss occurs within 4–5 years in 40% of all cases.
• Hair loss may follow some illnesses.

Get professional help if:
• Scalp looks red or scaly.
• Hair shafts are brittle or thick.
• Hair loss is diffuse rather than in clear patches.

Supplies: none.

Symptoms:
• bald patches on scalp

What to check:
• If hair and scalp look unhealthy, you cannot expect the hair to regrow on its own. Consult your doctor.
• Is hair being mistreated? Tight braids or ponytails or hair pulling can also cause hair loss.

Treatment:
• There is no home treatment for temporary hair loss.

Related topics: Thyroid Problem.

HAND, FOOT AND MOUTH DISEASE

Description: a viral infection causing sores in the mouth and blisters on hands and feet.

What you need to know:
• This disease lasts 3-7 days and disappears on its own.
• Key to diagnosis is the combination of mouth lesions and blisters on hands and feet.

Get professional help if:
• You aren't sure of the diagnosis.
• Your infant gets this disease.

Supplies: thermometer, aspirin (ASA)/acetaminophen (acet.), cool liquids, Popsicles.

Symptoms:
• blisters and shallow sores on mouth, cheeks, tongue, lips, throat
• blisters *also* on fingers, hands, toes, feet
• fever*
• headache
• sore muscles

What to check:
• If lesions first appear after taking a new medication, the problem may be an allergy. Check with your doctor.
• Large white patches on the roof of the mouth indicate thrush. Bad breath with mouth lesions indicate trench mouth. Check with your doctor.

Treatment:
• The object of home treatment is to make your child comfortable until the disease goes away.
• Give ASA/acet. to reduce soreness, fever.
• Urge your child to drink as much liquid as possible. Tart juices will be painful to drink.

Cool liquids, including Popsicles, are better.

Related topics: Blister, Cold Sore/Fever Blister.

*See Fever Guide, p. 27.

HAY FEVER

Description: stuffy nose, sneezing and itchy eyes caused by allergy to pollen, dust, dander or pets.

What you need to know:
• Hay fever is the most common allergic response.
• Dust and food cause most hay fever in infants.
• Dust and pollens cause most hay fever in older children.
• Seasonal hay fever is usually caused by ragweed pollen.

Get professional help if:
• The discomfort is great enough to warrant undertaking a program to reduce the child's sensitivity to some allergens.
• You think your child has asthma.

Supplies: OTC or prescribed antihistamines, decongestants, air conditioner, vacuum.

Symptoms:
• nasal congestion
• sneezing, with clear discharge
• itchy, irritated eyes
• headache

What to check:
• Membranes inside the nose will be pale instead of healthy pink.
• If symptoms coincide with pollen season, suspect hay fever. If symptoms are perennial, suspect some other allergy.

Treatment:
• Relieve symptoms with oral antihistamines or decongestants prescribed by your doctor.
• Reduce child's exposure to dust and pollen. Keep windows closed and use an air conditioner. Vacuum frequently and remove rugs, stuffed toys and other objects that could hold pollen.
• Use pillows stuffed only with synthetic material, such as polyester or foam rubber.

Related topics: Allergy, Asthma.

HEADACHE

Description: head pain; often it is a symptom of some other condition.

What you need to know:
• Headaches are a common childhood complaint; 95% of them are caused by fever,* strong emotions and stress.
• They rarely indicate a serious problem.

Get professional help if:
• Headaches increase in frequency or intensity, persist more than 3 days or follow head injury.
• Disorientation, vomiting, irritability, purple spotted rash or stiff neck also occur.
• A child age 4 or less complains of headache.

Supplies: thermometer, aspirin (ASA)/acetaminophen (acet.), prescribed medication (often antihistamines, nose drops).

Symptoms:
• pain, aching; it may be general or localized
• fussiness, irritability, crying in infants

What to check:
• Has the child recently been given a medication (such as decongestant, antihistamine) that may be causing pain?
• Look for causes: sinusitis, blows to the head.

Treatment:
• Give ASA/acet. for pain.
• If child's nose is also stuffy, try antihistamine or nose drops (but remember these may also *cause* headache).
• Give the child a neck massage, reassure and cuddle him. This may be particularly effective if headache is from stress or emotions.

• Reduce the causes of tension that may lead to headaches.

Related topics: Cold, Earache, Encephalitis, Sinusitis, Strep Throat.

*See Fever Guide, p. 27.

HEAD LICE

Description: tiny parasites living on or near the scalp, causing scalp itching and irritation.

What you need to know:
- Lice live only on humans, not pets.
- School children often acquire lice.
- It is best to treat all family members for lice if one member is infected.

Get professional help if:
- You suspect lice but cannot confirm their presence.
- Home treatment fails or works only temporarily.

Supplies: RID or other OTC preparation for killing lice, fine-tooth comb, hot water.

Symptoms:
- itching of the scalp
- scaly rash on back of neck near hairline
- enlarged lymph glands at base of skull

What to check:
- Lice are almost impossible to see.
- Eggs (nits) are more easily seen: they appear as white flecks on hair. Unlike dandruff, nits are firmly fastened to hair shafts.

Treatment:
- Procedures vary depending on which preparation is used. Most involve repeated shampoos, each followed by combing with a fine-tooth comb.
- Other family members should be treated to prevent reinfestation.
- Combs and hairbrushes should be treated with the preparation or with hot water.
- Hats and pillowcases should be cleaned in very hot water or dry cleaned.

HEARING LOSS

Description: partial or total loss of hearing resulting from congenital defect, illness or injury.

What you need to know:
• Sudden loss of hearing is usually temporary and probably indicates blockage of the eardrum by a foreign object, infection or wax.
• A history of deafness in your family should increase your suspicions of hearing loss in your child.

Get professional help if:
• Hearing loss persists more than 1 week or is combined with fever* or earache.
• A 3-month-old baby does not respond to sound.
• A child does not begin to use a few words by age 1 or form 3-word sentences by age 3.
• A school-age child has learning problems.

Supplies: thermometer, prescribed medication.

Symptoms:
• lack of response to sounds
• failure to talk/slow speech development
• dizziness
• difficulty with balance, coordination
• pain or ringing in ears

What to check:
• Does child have problems at school (difficulty learning or paying attention, disruptiveness)?
• Does the child talk loudly, not respond when spoken to, turn the TV to a high volume or sit close to it?

Treatment:
• All conditions that cause earache or hearing loss should be treated by a doctor.
• Do not attempt to remove a foreign object from the ear; see a doctor.
• Do not insert an object —even a cotton swab—into the ear to remove wax. See your doctor if you cannot remove wax with a washcloth.

Related topics: Earache, Ear Injury.

*See Fever Guide, p. 27.

HEAT EXHAUSTION (PROSTRATION)

Description: a condition that occurs when the body overheats due to excessive heat in the environment and/or overexertion.

What you need to know:
- Heat exhaustion is *not* a medical emergency but does require prompt attention.
- It can follow normal exertion in a hot environment or overexertion in moderate temperatures.
- It is different from heat stroke (see p. 132).

Get professional help if:
- Symptoms last more than 1 hour or worsen.
- Your child is suffering from another illness.

Supplies: thermometer, cool salt water (1 tsp./glass), other cool liquids, cool compresses, or cool water and a sponge or washcloth.

Symptoms:
- pale, clammy skin
- excessive sweating
- headache/dizziness
- nausea/thirst
- fatigue/weakness
- possibly cramps, fainting, vomiting
- near-normal temperature*

What to check:
- Is temperature near normal? If it is elevated, heat stroke may be possible.
- Has child been in the sun or a hot environment for a long time?
- Has he been physically active in a hot *or* temperate environment?

Treatment:
- Have child lie down in a cool, shady area. Loosen or remove clothes.
- Elevate feet slightly.
- If he can swallow, give salt water or cool liquids in sips.
- Apply cool compresses to forehead/body or sponge with cool water.

Related topics: Heat Stroke, Unconsciousness.

*See Fever Guide, p. 27.

HEAT RASH (PRICKLY HEAT)

Description: small red bumps in skin folds, especially likely to occur on neck and upper chest of newborn.

What you need to know:
• Heat rash is very common and causes only minor discomfort.
• Problem is caused by the blockage of pores leading to sweat glands.

Get professional help if:
• Blisters appear on the bumps.

Supplies: cool baths, baby powder.

Symptoms:
• many tiny red bumps in folds of skin
• most often seen on cheeks, neck, shoulders, creases in skin and diaper area

What to check:
• Is laundry thoroughly rinsed? Some detergents and bleaches aggravate heat rash.
• Is the baby overdressed? It may contribute to heat rash.
• Are oily skin products blocking pores?

Treatment:
• Keep baby's skin as cool and dry as possible.
• Give frequent cool baths to help open skin pores.
• Dress the infant as lightly as possible in natural fibers.
• Put the infant in an air conditioned environment if possible.

• Apply baby powder to keep skin dry.

Related topics: Diaper Rash.

HEAT STROKE (SUNSTROKE)

Description: a life-threatening condition due to a failure of the body's temperature-regulating ability, caused by extreme heat.

What you need to know:
- Unlike heat exhaustion, heat stroke is a medical emergency. It can be fatal if not treated promptly.
- Children in moderate climates are particularly susceptible during heat waves.

Get professional help if:
- Your child shows symptoms of heat stroke.

Supplies: thermometer, tub of cold water, hose, cold packs, sponge, alcohol.

Symptoms:
- extremely high temperature (105°F.)*
- no sweating
- hot, flushed skin
- unconsciousness or confusion

What to check:
- Has your child been exposed to extremely hot temperatures, even without physical exertion?

Treatment:
- Remove child from direct sunlight; undress her. Get help.
- Try to lower temperature quickly. Place her in a tub of cold (not ice) water, or hose her, apply cold packs or sponge with alcohol or cold water. Continue cooling until temperature drops to 101°F.
- Lay child down with legs somewhat elevated and continue cooling procedures.
- Do *not* give stimulants (cola, coffee, tea) or alcoholic drinks.

Related topics: Fever, Heat Exhaustion, Unconsciousness.

*See Fever Guide, p. 27.

HEPATITIS

Description: a viral disease of the liver.

What you need to know:
• Hepatitis is a common disease in children and is usually so mild it goes unnoticed.
• Hepatitis exists in many forms, which differ mostly in how they are transmitted.

Get professional help if:
• Hepatitis is suspected. It is important to protect other family members with gamma globulin shots to reduce the severity of the symptoms if they get hepatitis.

Supplies: liquids, low-fat diet.

Symptoms:
• marked loss of appetite
• nausea, vomiting
• liver pain (upper-right quarter of the abdomen).
• jaundice (yellowish tinge to skin and whites of eyes)

What to check:
• Is there liver pain (tenderness in the upper-right quarter of the abdomen)?

Treatment:
• As soon as you suspect hepatitis, isolate the sick child (and his dishes, glasses, silverware) from the rest of the family and call your doctor.
• Your doctor will determine a program of treatment. Usually the sick child is given plenty of rest and liquids and is put on a low-fat diet.

Related topics: Jaundice in Newborns.

HERNIA

Description: the protrusion of an organ through the wall of a body cavity.

What you need to know:
• Hernias are common, affecting 5% of all children.
• Some hernias are self-healing and harmless, while strangulated hernias are medical emergencies.
• Umbilical hernias (around the navel) are not serious, are often self-healing, and do not require home treatment.

Supplies: thermometer.

Get professional help if:
• A hernia won't go back into body if pushed gently. *Seek help immediately.*
• Child has fever,* severe pain, nausea or vomiting.
• The hernia occurs in an infant (the younger the child, the more urgent the need for help). All hernias should be checked.

Symptoms:
• bulges in the groin or abdomen that may appear and disappear as the child strains and relaxes
• sometimes, swelling of the scrotal sac in boys

What to check:
• Check hernia's response to a gentle push. If it won't go back into body, seek help immediately; if it does, call your doctor for an appointment.
• Check for a bulge if your child suddenly begins crying as if in pain.

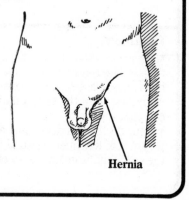

Hernia

Treatment:
• Most hernias that need treatment are handled surgically.
• Trusses and belts to hold hernias in are considered useless or dangerous.

Related topics: Testicle, Torsion of.

* See Fever Guide, p. 27.

HERPES STOMATITIS

Description: an oral infection seen in toddlers' mouths, caused by the herpes simplex virus.

What you need to know:
• This infection occurs only once in its oral form.
• It is seen mostly among children of preschool age.
• It does not have a common name.

Get professional help if:
• Your child refuses all liquids for longer than 12 hours.
• The disease seems to recur.

Supplies: thermometer, penlight, aspirin (ASA)/acetaminophen (acet.), non-carbonated, non-tart liquids.

Symptoms:
• blisters on the tongue, gums, inside of cheeks
• temperature of 102–103°F.*
• loss of appetite
• drooling

What to check:
• Use penlight to look into child's mouth. Are blisters visible?

Treatment:
• Give ASA/acet. for pain and fever.
• Offer non-carbonated, non-tart liquids, such as water, milk and malts.

Related topics: Cold Sore/Fever Blister; Hand, Foot and Mouth Disease.

*See Fever Guide, p. 27.

HIGH BLOOD PRESSURE

Description: an elevation of blood pressure above normal ranges.

What you need to know:
• High blood pressure (hypertension) almost never has apparent symptoms. It can affect people of any age.
• Your child should have his blood pressure checked at his regular checkups. (See pp. 14–15 for schedule.)

Get professional help if:
• Unexplained numbness of your child's arms or face occurs.
• Heart palpitation (irregular, fast beats), skipped beat or shortness of breath occurs.

Supplies: none.

Symptoms:
• In severe cases, these symptoms may occur:
–numb arms or face
–black-out spells, dizziness, blurred or lost vision, fatigue, weakness
–paralysis, twitching
–headache, irritability, insomnia

What to check:
• Have your child's blood pressure checked regularly.
• Is your child overweight, consuming too much salt, not getting enough exercise?

Treatment:
• Consult your doctor immediately if you suspect your child might have elevated blood pressure.

Related topics: Headache, Nose Bleed

HIP PROBLEM

Description: hip or knee pain from several possible sources, causing child to limp or refuse to walk.

What you need to know:

• Hip pain is a common childhood complaint that may indicate mild irritation or point to a severe problem.
• A variety of conditions can cause hip pain; your doctor can determine which is the source of the problem.

Get professional help if:

• Child complains of persistent pain or limps when there is no obvious cause.
• Fever* accompanies hip pain. *Call your doctor immediately.*
• Pain is severe.
• Pain persists more than 1 day.

Supplies: thermometer, warm baths.

Symptoms:

• hip, knee pain
• limp
• infant refuses to walk or cries if urged to walk
• fever*

What to check:

• Check for fever.
• Knee pain often originates in the hip. Examine hip for full range of motion. Don't force any movement.

Treatment:

• Warm baths and rest will relieve pain of minor hip problems.

Related topics: Arthritis, Knee Pain.

* See Fever Guide, p. 27.

HIVES

Description: an allergic reaction of the skin appearing as many red, raised, itchy welts.

What you need to know:
- Hives affect 20% of all children at least once.
- Most hives disappear on their own in several days.
- Hives may be caused by many things: insect bites, medications, foods, pet saliva, viruses, weather changes.

Get professional help if:
- Mouth or inside of throat is affected. If breathing is hindered, *call your doctor immediately.*
- Fever* accompanies attack.
- Symptoms are severe.
- Antihistamines don't help.

Supplies: thermometer, OTC or prescribed antihistamines, ice water compresses.

Symptoms:
- many red bumps in skin
- individual bumps come and go. If an individual welt stays more than 12 hours, the rash is *not* hives

What to check:
- If hives are accompanied by a fever, see your doctor to make sure the child does not have strep throat.

Treatment:
- Determine, if possible, what caused the reaction. The first line of treatment should be to avoid further exposure to the cause.
- Administer antihistamines as directed.
- Use ice water compresses to relieve itching.

- You can leave mild attacks untreated, since they are self-curing.

Related topics: Allergy; Bites and Stings, Insect.

*See Fever Guide, p. 27.

HYPERACTIVITY

Description: an excessively high activity level that may contribute to behavior problems.

What you need to know:
• Hyperactivity is not a disease but a symptom of some kind of problem.
• It must be diagnosed with great care because there is no real standard for a "normal" activity level in children.

Get professional help if:
• You suspect your child is hyperactive. Consider talking to your doctor if your child's activity level seems to be causing problems for the child (poor performance at school) or for family members at home.

Supplies: none.

Symptoms:
• markedly high activity levels
• poor concentration
• wild mood swings
• lack of coordination
• learning problems
• (note: all these symptoms are relative and must be evaluated in context)

What to check:
• Has your child suddenly developed symptoms of hyperactivity after taking a new medication? If so, talk to your doctor right away.

Treatment:
• Diagnosis and treatment of hyperactivity must be done by a physician. Under no circumstances should a parent administer drugs in an effort to control what seems to be hyperactivity.

HYPERVENTILATION

Description: excessively rapid breathing, leading to numbness, dizziness, chest pain or panic.

What you need to know:
- Hyperventilation is caused by stress.
- Rapid breathing lowers the level of carbon dioxide in the blood, causing tingling symptoms.
- The syndrome is common with older children.

Get professional help if:
- Symptoms persist despite home treatment.

Supplies: paper bag.

Symptoms:
- rapid breathing
- numbness or tingling in hands, feet and mouth
- panic at apparent inability to breathe
- tight, restricted feeling in chest

What to check:
- Hyperventilation is a response to stress. It may indicate stress due to family, school or personal difficulties.

Treatment:
- Have your child breathe into a paper bag or cupped hands held loosely around the nose and mouth until carbon dioxide level rises and breathing is normal (usually about 10 minutes).
- Reassure her that hyperventilation isn't serious. Explain how hyperventilation works after she is calmed and explore the underlying emotional problems that led to it.

Related topics: Chest Pain, Unconsciousness.

HYPOGLYCEMIA

Description: a metabolic condition in which the level of sugar in the blood is low.

What you need to know:

• It is most common in children from age 1 to 6 who are below average in height and weight, who have small appetites and who are very active.
• It may result from prolonged undereating or vomiting or be related to other conditions.

Get professional help if:

• You suspect your child has hypoglycemia. A doctor's diagnosis and prescribed treatment are needed.
• Symptoms do not disappear with treatment.
• Your diabetic child shows symptoms of hypoglycemia (here, insulin shock).

Supplies: foods high in protein, complex carbohydrates and simple sugars (fruits, vegetables, whole grain breads, cereals, potatoes).

Symptoms:

• dizziness, faintness
• sweating, cool skin
• irritability, nervousness
• paleness
• headache
• fatigue, drowsiness
• hunger

What to check:

• Watch for loss of appetite in diagnosed hypoglycemic children when they are ill.

Treatment:

• Follow your doctor's prescribed program of treatment. It may include:
– increasing the amount of calories in meals.
– giving snacks high in complex carbohydrates (but *not* refined sugar, as in candy or pop)
– increasing calories and carbohydrates on days when the child is very active.

Related topics: Diabetes, Headache, Unconsciousness.

HYPOTHERMIA

Description: severe heat loss leading to dangerously low core body temperatures.

What you need to know:
• Hypothermia can be fatal. Symptoms of hypothermia are easily missed.
• Bodies lose heat much faster in cold water or through wet clothing than when dry.

Get professional help if:
• Your child loses consciousness due to hypothermia.
• Your child's temperature falls below 94°F.
• Symptoms persist despite home treatment.

Supplies: thermometer, tub of warm water, towels, warm blankets, warm sweet drinks or soup (no alcoholic beverages).

Symptoms:
• extreme, uncontrollable shivering
• slurred speech/confusion
• exhaustion/drowsiness
• loss of strength, coordination
• impaired judgment

What to check:
• Hypothermia can occur together with frostbite. Be careful to avoid injuring frostbitten body parts when warming a child suffering from heat loss.

Treatment:
• Get your child out of cold, wet clothing and into a warm room. Keep him awake.
• Bring body temperature up quickly by placing the child in a tub of water that's warm to the elbow.
• Or wrap the child in warm blankets, preferably with another person, to gain from body-to-body warmth.
• Give warm drinks to the child only if he is conscious.

Related topics: Frostbite.

IMPETIGO

Description: contagious abscesses on the skin, caused by bacteria.

What you need to know:
• Impetigo is contagious, spreading readily from one part of the body to another or from child to child through contact.
• Though not serious, it must be treated with care and persistence.

Get professional help if:
• Impetigo seems to be spreading or not responding to home treatment after 5 days.
• Your child develops symptoms of glomerulonephritis, a rare kidney complication of impetigo (see symptoms below).

Supplies: soap and water, compress, OTC antibiotic ointment, nail clipper.

Symptoms:
• yellowish scabs on the surface of the skin, often occurring in groups, with or without oozing fluid
• cola-colored urine and a headache (symptoms of glomerulonephritis).

What to check:
• Since impetigo is contagious, check other family members for signs of infection.
• Make sure each family member uses his or her own towel and washcloth.

Treatment:
• Clean the skin with soap and water, then soak sores with a compress for 10 minutes.
• Rub away the crust and pus when the crust softens.
• Cover sores with antibiotic cream 3 times a day.
• Continue treatment 3–4 times a day until all sores lose their scabs.
• Clip your child's nails to discourage scratching, as this spreads the disease.

Related topics: Blisters.

INFLUENZA

Description: a viral infection of the respiratory tract that causes fever, chills, cough, and aches.

What you need to know:
• Like the common cold, flu can't be avoided, has no cure, is uncomfortable but not serious. It often lasts 3–4 days, but may last a week. Children weakened by flu can catch other diseases.
• Use of aspirin for influenza may be related to the development of Reye's syndrome (p. 173).

Get professional help if:
• Complications occur. Common examples are return of fever, worsening cough, pneumonia, ear infections and sinusitis.
• Your child has diabetes, severe asthma or another chronic disease. Your doctor may want to give him flu shots.

Supplies: thermometer, acetaminophen (acet.)—*not* aspirin (ASA), cough medications.

Symptoms:
• fever*
• chills
• cough
• muscle aches
• headache
• fatigue
• in young children, diarrhea and vomiting

What to check:
• Watch for complications.
• Check fever. With some children fever has two peaks, separated by a day of normal temperatures.

Treatment:
• Treatment is aimed at giving child rest while relieving pain of symptoms.
• Bedrest, acet. and consumption of fluids are recommended.
• Don't let child become active after only one feverless day.
• Give cough medications to children suffering pain or loss of sleep from a cough.
• Isolate the sick child because the disease is highly contagious.

Related topics: Cough, Diarrhea, Headache, Reye's Syndrome, Sore Muscle, Vomiting.

*See Fever Guide, p. 27.

INGROWN TOENAIL

Description: a toenail that penetrates the nearby skin, causing pain and swelling.

What you need to know:

- Most cases involve the big toe of older children.
- Overly tight shoes, clipping toenails too short and accidents may cause the condition.
- Regular nail cutting helps prevent ingrown toenails.

Get professional help if:

- The nail penetrates the skin.
- There is sign of infection (pus, swelling, redness).

Supplies: warm water, cotton, nail clippers, Epsom salt, bandage, plastic bag.

Symptoms:

- tenderness
- redness
- pain, usually localized on one side of nail

What to check:

- Shoe length and width. Tightness may not bother your child, but may cause ingrown toenails.
- Is your child trimming nails straight across with no sharp edges?

Treatment:

- Soak his foot in warm water for 30 minutes, then gently lift the ingrown part and push cotton underneath to separate from tender skin.

- After nail is trimmed, soak foot in Epsom salt (1 c./1 qt. warm water) for 2–3 hours for several days.
- Or put bandage soaked in Epsom salt on foot, put foot in plastic bag and bind loosely for bedtime treatment.

JAUNDICE IN NEWBORNS

Description: a symptom, not a disease, characterized by a yellow tinge to the skin and eyes.

What you need to know:
- Mild degree of jaundice is common in newborns. It usually appears in the the second or third day of life and lasts until end of the baby's first week.
- Severe jaundice or jaundice in older children is cause for concern (see p. 133).

Get professional help if:
- Symptoms appear in *first* 24 hours of life.
- Jaundice develops or worsens after newborn leaves the hospital.
- Jaundice occurs in older children.

Supplies: none.

Symptoms:
- skin color is yellow
- eye whites are yellow

What to check:
- Newborn should be observed carefully in first week at home.
- Check newborn in natural light; artificial light obscures true color.

Treatment:
- Mild jaundice may improve if newborn is exposed to sunlight (not too much).
- Some jaundice in newborns is caused by a hormone in the mother's milk. It may be necessary to stop nursing the baby, at least temporarily, and give supplemental water.

Related topics: Hepatitis.

KNEE PAIN

Description: pain in knee, often accompanied by swelling or loss of normal range of movement.

What you need to know:
- Most knee pain results from trauma and quickly disappears.
- Some knee pain indicates serious problems, such as rheumatoid arthritis, ligament or cartilage damage, or other disorders.

Get professional help if:
- Skin is swollen over the knees.
- Pain is severe.
- Fever* is present.
- Pain persists or returns after disappearing.
- Knee movement is limited or abnormal.

Supplies: ice, elastic, knee support.

Symptoms:
- pain or tenderness
- limping
- loss of movement in joint
- abnormal side-to-side movement
- swelling

What to check:
- Check knee movement gently.
- Knee pain may indicate hip problems. Check hip movement.

Treatment:
- Mild knee pain from minor trauma can be treated at home by giving him rest, elevating the leg and applying ice.

- Take your child to a doctor *immediately* if you suspect serious problems.
- An elastic bandage can help him avoid bending knee until it is well.

Related topics: Arthritis, Hip Problem.

*See Fever Guide, p. 27.

147

LARYNGITIS

Description: an inflammation of the voice box, causing hoarseness, coughing, throat pain.

What you need to know:
• Laryngitis is a self-limiting illness, rarely lasting more than 48 hours.
• It is one of the diseases most resistant to therapy.
• It usually comes as the last phase of some colds.
• Laryngitis is not cause for alarm unless your child has problems breathing. ·

Get professional help if:
• Your child has any difficulty breathing. *Get help immediately.*
• Laryngitis is accompanied by a climbing fever or croupy cough.
• Your child drools a lot.
• Hoarseness lasts longer than a week.

Supplies: thermometer, cool mist vaporizer, warm liquids, cough medicine, aspirin (ASA)/acetaminophen (acet.).

Symptoms:
• hoarseness/loss of voice
• dry, hacking cough
• low-grade fever*
• sore throat

What to check:
• Monitor temperature.
• Watch for symptoms of croup (see p. 96).

Treatment:
• Keep child in a room with a vaporizer.
• Urge child to drink warm liquids.
• Discourage talking, and especially crying, by whispering to the child.
• Give cough medicine to relieve coughing.

• Use ASA/acet. to reduce fever and throat pain.

Related topics: Croup, Epiglottitis.

*See Fever Guide, p. 27.

LEG PAIN AT NIGHT

Description: muscle aches in the leg, usually felt most acutely at night.

What you need to know:

• The combined stress of rapid growth and vigorous activity can cause leg pains.
• These usually occur at night, sometimes waking the child.
• Most such pains can be regarded as normal "growing pains."

Get professional help if:

• The pains are severe or persistent.
• Your child had a sore throat several weeks before the onset of the pains.
• The pain is in the *joints,* not the muscles.
• Any swelling appears in the legs or leg joints.

Supplies: aspirin (ASA)/acetaminophen (acet.), warm compresses or heating pads.

Symptoms:

• aching, usually in the middle of the muscles of the lower or upper leg
• usually both legs or both feet hurt

What to check:

• Has your child recently had a sore throat, possibly strep? If so, see your doctor. Strep throat can lead to rheumatic fever and be expressed as leg pain, but this is rare. Almost always, night leg pain is harmless.

Treatment:

• Give ASA/acet. to relieve the muscle pain.
• Some children find warm compresses or heating pads helpful.

Related topics: Sore Muscle.

LEUKEMIA

Description: cancer of the white blood cells.

What you need to know:
• Leukemia, though rare, is a serious disease that can be fatal.
• New therapies have dramatically improved chances for remission or cure of leukemia.

Get professional help if:
• You suspect your child has leukemia.

Supplies: thermometer.

Symptoms:
• anemia/paleness
• spontaneous body bruises
• swollen, red gums
• low-grade fever*
• bone, joint pain
• frequent, recurring, uncontrollable nosebleeds
• blood in urine or stools

What to check:
• If a *number* of the listed symptoms seem to be present, check with your doctor.
• Any *one* of the listed symptoms is most likely *not* due to leukemia, but some other, much less serious problem.

Treatment:
• Leukemia must be treated by a physician, preferably a specialist operating from a cancer or leukemia treatment center.

*See Fever Guide, p. 27.

MEASLES

Description: a highly contagious viral illness with fever, runny nose, cough and red-spotted rash.

What you need to know:
- Infants are immune until about the first birthday; *they should be immunized at 15 months.*
- While measles disappears on its own in about 7 days, it can lead to complications. Unvaccinated children exposed to measles can be protected with gamma globulin shots.

Get professional help if:
- An unvaccinated child is exposed to measles.
- Fever and cough do not subside after the rash peaks.
- The cough lasts more than 4 days; this could be pneumonia.
- Child has ear pain or becomes lethargic.
- Breathing difficulty, vomiting or disorientation appear.

Supplies: thermometer, aspirin (ASA)/acetaminophen (acet.), cough medicine, fluids.

Symptoms:
- same as bad cold at first (cough, red/watery eyes, low-grade fever*)
- fever rises sharply on fourth day and rash appears, starting on face and neck before moving down to rest of body
- eyes sensitive to light

What to check:
- Watch for complications (above).

Treatment:
- Exposed children develop symptoms 10–12 days later. They are contagious until after the third day of the rash.
- Give ASA/acet. to reduce fever.
- Give cough medicine for coughing.

- Offer lots of fluids.
- Since children with measles are sensitive to light, you should keep your child in a darkened room for comfort.
- Call your doctor if complications appear.

Related topics: Pinkeye.

*See Fever Guide, p. 27.

MENINGITIS

Description: a bacterial or viral infection of the membranes surrounding the brain and spinal cord.

What you need to know:
• Meningitis is a serious disease that should be diagnosed and treated by a physician *as soon as possible.*
• Untreated meningitis can lead to impaired brain function or even death.

Get professional help if:
• Meningitis symptoms are noted. No single symptom is indicative; look for the combination of symptoms listed.
• If you are unsure or concerned, call your doctor.

Supplies: thermometer.

Symptoms:
• moderate to high fever*
• severe headache
• vomiting
• prostration, lethargy
• stiff neck (sometimes not in infants)
• purple spots on body (sometimes)

What to check:
• If your child appears to have acquired meningitis through contact with someone with the illness, try to learn the cause of that person's meningitis (virus or bacteria).

Treatment:
• Meningitis is a serious disease. It should always be treated by a physician. See your doctor *immediately* if you suspect meningitis.

Related topics: Headache, Vomiting.

*See Fever Guide, p. 27.

MENSTRUAL IRREGULARITY

Description: irregular flow in the early years of menstruation.

What you need to know:
• Periods are likely to be irregular when a girl starts menstruating. Girls have many more concerns than actual problems with early periods, partly because they haven't been told how variable the experience is.

Get professional help if:
• The first period occurs before age 9 or has not occurred by age 16.
• Periods are extremely heavy, painful, frequent, or prolonged.
• Periods stop for 4 months or longer.

Supplies: aspirin (ASA)/acetaminophen (acet.).

Symptoms:
• cramping
• headache
• nausea
• irritability

What to check:
• Ask your daughter to keep a log of her periods and to note the days when she feels discomfort. This will aid your doctor in deciding what treatment, if any, is necessary.

Treatment:
• Talk to your daughter well before she needs information about menstruation. Information and trust are the cures for most concerns about menstruation. Don't count on the school system to meet this responsibility.

• Give ASA/acet. for discomfort.

MOLE

Description: benign skin tumors appearing as small brown, black, or flesh-colored spots, usually the size of freckles.

What you need to know:
- Moles are common. At birth, 2% of white babies and 20% of black babies have moles. Almost all children develop them later.
- They rarely are harmful, though some become malignant.

Get professional help if:
- A mole enlarges rapidly, develops a sore, bleeds or changes color.
- A mole has been partly removed by accident.

Supplies: none.

Signs:
- small black, brown or flesh-colored spots or lumps
- usually they do not disappear
- sometimes a halo or coloring develops around the mole and then disappears

What to check:
- If your child is born with a mole, talk to your doctor about having it removed.

Treatment:
- Almost all moles are harmless and require no treatment. Moles present at birth are the only type that should be removed for health reasons.
- Objectionable moles can be removed for cosmetic reasons.
- It may be desirable to remove a mole that is located on a part of the body where it is bumped or irritated frequently.

Related topics: Birthmark.

MOLLUSCUM CONTAGIOSUM

Description: a viral skin infection that appears as raised, waxy, pimple-like nodules.

What you need to know:
• Though it is common and harmless, it is very contagious, being spread by direct contact with the skin or through contact with clothing or towels used by an infected person.

Get professional help if:
• The infection does not resolve itself after 1 month.
• The spread of infection continues through the family.

Supplies: none.

Symptoms:
• one or many round, raised, waxy pimples on skin that resemble miniature volcanoes

What to check:
• Has the infection lasted more than a month?
• Are other family members protected?

Treatment:
• No treatment of the skin is necessary unless the infection persists for more than a month, and then a doctor's treatment is necessary.
• Protect other members of the family by limiting contact between them and the infected child. Isolate her clothing and towels until laundering, which kills the virus.

MONONUCLEOSIS

Description: a viral illness that causes cold-like symptoms, sore throat, fatigue and malaise.

What you need to know:
- It is a common disease of children and young adults.
- Children with mono may have few or no symptoms, while adolescents may be ill for many weeks or longer.
- Mono cannot be cured, but goes away on its own.

Get professional help if:
- Your child develops symptoms that suggest mono. The illness resembles many others. A blood test will confirm mono.
- A child with mono also has trouble breathing or abdominal pain.

Supplies: thermometer, aspirin (ASA)/acetaminophen (acet.) throat lozenges.

Symptoms:
- fever*
- sore throat
- loss of appetite
- sleepiness
- headache
- general malaise
- swollen lymph nodes

What to check:
- Look for any signs of obstructed breathing, a rare but serious complication. If it appears, *see a doctor immediately.*

Treatment:
- A sick child will want bed-rest. When the child again wants to be active, it will be safe to allow that.
- Treat fever and throat pain with ASA/acet.
- Throat lozenges or medication will ease throat pain.
- Isolate the sick child from other family members while cold symptoms persist, and don't allow contact sports during that time due to the slight risk of a ruptured spleen.

Related topics: Headache, Sore Throat, Tonsilitis.

*See Fever Guide, p. 27.

MOTION SICKNESS

Description: nausea caused by the rhythmic motion of air, sea, or car travel.

What you need to know:	Get professional help if:
• Motion sickness is not the fault of the child. • Some children are much more inclined than others to motion sickness. • Prolonged vomiting can lead to dehydration or even vomiting blood.	• Severe, protracted vomiting causes dehydration or vomiting blood. • Occurrence of motion sickness is regular enough to require medication.

Supplies: games, OTC antinauseant medication (Dramamine).

Symptoms:	What to check:
• nausea • pale or green skin color • vomiting • perspiration	• Make sure some other illness is not the cause of the vomiting.
Treatment: • Reduce the chances your child will become sick. Avoid heavy meals before trips. Fresh air (no smoking) helps. Put the child in front car seat, rear boat seat or over plane wing. Direct attention forward to horizon rather than sides. Don't allow the child to read.	• Preoccupy the child with games. • Give antinauseant an hour before trip and every 4 hours during the trip (check dosage amount with physician).

Related topics: Vomiting.

MOUTH/TOOTH INJURY

Description: injuries to the gums, palate, teeth, lips and tongue.

What you need to know:
• Dislodged or loosened permanent teeth can sometimes be replaced.
• Bring broken or dislodged tooth to your dentist. If your child is old enough, ask him to carry the tooth in his mouth. Otherwise wrap it in a clean, moist cloth.

Supplies: sterile gauze, ice.

Get professional help if:
• A tooth is dislodged, loosened or broken. A chipped tooth is painful. See your dentist immediately.
• An object or tooth has been impaled in mouth tissue.
• Bleeding is extensive.
• A cut needs to be stitched.

Symptoms:
• bleeding
• swelling

What to check:
• Are there any head or neck injuries? Sometimes they occur as part of the accident that causes mouth or tooth injuries.

Treatment:
• If there is bleeding, have your child lean forward slightly to avoid inhaling blood.
• Control gum bleeding by pressing gauze tightly to injury or applying ice.
• Control tooth bleeding by biting firmly on gauze.
• Control lip bleeding by pinching injured spot firmly with gauze.
• Control tongue bleeding by pressing both sides with gauze.

Related topics: Cut/Wound.

MUMPS

Description: a mild and common viral illness that affects the salivary glands.

What you need to know:
- Mumps can be prevented by vaccination. *Get your child immunized.*
- Infants enjoy immunity until their first birthday.
- Mumps confers its own immunity. Some cases are so mild they go unnoted.
- Adult cases can be painful.

Get professional help if:
- Your child with mumps suddenly gets a headache, is nauseated, vomits, or has severe stomach or testicular pain.
- An adult appears to have contracted mumps from a child.

Supplies: thermometer, aspirin (ASA)/acetaminophen (acet.), cold compresses.

Symptoms:
- swelling of salivary glands (swelling will center in front of earlobes) on one or both sides
- fever,* usually low-grade
- loss of appetite

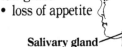

Salivary gland
Lymph nodes

What to check:
- Don't confuse mumps with swollen lymph glands (see p. 199). Mumps make it hard to feel the jawline and make swallowing and chewing painful.

Treatment:
- There is no cure, so treatment is aimed at symptoms. Contagious phase starts before the swelling begins and lasts 10 days.
- Give ASA/acet. for pain and fever; use cold compresses on forehead for headaches.
- Urge your child to stay in bed at first. She will feel better and will not expose others. But when she feels like being active again, she is probably ready.
- Avoid spicy, sour foods.

Related topics: Swollen Lymph Gland.

*See Fever Guide, p. 27.

NEPHRITIS

Description: an inflammation of the kidney.

What you need to know:
• Nephritis may follow 1-3 weeks after strep throat, scarlet fever or streptococcal impetigo.
• Usually mild, it cannot be treated and goes away on its own in several weeks. But it can be severe or become chronic.

Get professional help if:
• The symptoms of nephritis are detected. Most cases go undetected; if symptoms *are* noted, your child is ill enough to be taken to your doctor as soon as possible.

Supplies: thermometer.

Symptoms:
• puffiness around eyes
• red, or cola-colored urine
• loss of appetite
• fever*
• headache
• decreased urine output
• vomiting

What to check:
• Be alert for symptoms if your child has had impetigo, scarlet fever or strep throat.

Treatment:
• Nephritis that produces observable symptoms requires a doctor's diagnosis and treatment. Some forms are severe and chronic, requiring kidney dialysis therapy or a kidney transplant.

Related topics: Headache, Strep Throat.

*See Fever Guide, p. 27.

NOSEBLEED

Description: bleeding from the nose, from blood vessels in the nasal passages.

What you need to know:
• Nosebleeds are common because the tiny vessels in the nose break easily.
• Dry air, frequent nose blowing or picking, or blows to the nose cause most nosebleeds.
• Blood loss is usually light.

Get professional help if:
• Bleeding persists longer than 30 minutes.
• There is a history of repeated bleeding from the same nostril.
• Nosebleeds occur frequently.
• There is a persistent drain of blood to the child's throat.
• Bleeding problems occur at other sites.

Supplies: medicated ointments (Bacitracin) or petroleum jelly, cool mist vaporizer.

Symptoms:
• blood coming from nose
• blood in throat or vomit (comes from nose, draining back into throat)

What to check:
• Be sure there is no foreign object in the nose.

Treatment:
• Calm your child; crying increases blood flow. Ask her to sit leaning slightly forward.
• Pinch nose, compressing whole soft portion for 10 minutes to allow clot to form.
• If treatment fails, try again, holding nose firmly for another 20 minutes.

• Ointments on nasal passages and use of vaporizer help prevent nosebleeds.

Related topics: Anemia, Nose Injury, Object in Nose.

NOSE INJURY

Description: injury to the nose causing bleeding, swelling, disfigurement or impaired breathing.

What you need to know:
- Few nose injuries cause problems needing immediate professional attention. Your doctor may prefer to see your child after the swelling has gone down.
- The symptoms are less severe if your child relaxes.

Get professional help if:
- The pain is extreme.
- The nose seems misshapen.
- The child has trouble breathing or can't breathe through each nostril separately (close one at a time with your finger).
- You detect infection.

Supplies: cold compress, aspirin (ASA)/acetaminophen (acet.).

.Symptoms:
- bleeding, swollen or disfigured nose

What to check:
- Look for swelling or foul discharge, indications of an infection.

Treatment:
- Stop bleeding with same procedures listed for nosebleed (see p. 161).
- Reduce swelling with cold compresses, then see your doctor.
- Offer ASA/acet. for pain.

Related topics: Nosebleed.

OBJECT IN NOSE

Description: a foreign object lodged within a nostril or more deeply inside the nose.

What you need to know:
• Small children may put objects in their nose.

Get professional help if:
• You cannot easily see and grasp the object. If it is inserted so far you cannot grasp it firmly, you risk pushing it in further by trying to remove it yourself.
• The nose is badly damaged.

Supplies: penlight, round-end tweezers.

Symptoms:
• bleeding from nose
• object visible in nose
• bad smelling, often blood-tinged, nasal discharge

What to check:
• Is the nasal discharge from one side of the nose only?
• Can you see anything inside the nose (use penlight)?

Treatment:
• Have her breathe through her mouth if she has any difficulty breathing.
• If she is old enough, have her blow her nose vigorously.
• Remove the object with round-end tweezers *only if you are sure you can do so safely and easily.*

• Prevent accidents by keeping small children from playing with tiny objects.

Related topics: Nosebleed.

PIERCED EAR INFECTION

Description: infection of the earlobe associated with pierced earrings or the piercing procedure.

What you need to know:	**Get professional help if:**
• Infections can result from too-short posts, sensitivity to metals, improper piercing procedures or improper care after piercing. • Never try to pierce your child's ears yourself.	• Infection is severe. • Home treatment does not improve the condition in a few days. • Eczema develops (see p. 108).

Supplies: rubbing alcohol, cotton balls, antibiotic ointment.

Symptoms:	**What to check:**
• swelling/tenderness/redness of area around the hole • rawness and discharge; discharge dries and forms itchy scales • lumps in earlobes	• Are earrings made of good-quality metals (gold, silver, stainless steel)? • Are posts so short they don't extend well beyond back of lobe? • Is clasp pushed on too tightly so it pinches ear?
Treatment: • Remove earrings until infection clears up. • Clean front and back of lobe twice daily with alcohol and apply antibiotic ointment. • The hole may grow closed in the healing process, requiring re-piercing.	• Proper procedures for caring for newly pierced ears are: –insert only post earrings and don't remove for 4-6 weeks. –clean front and back of lobe twice daily with alcohol and turn earrings several times daily.

PINKEYE

Description: an irritation of the linings of the eyelids and the coverings of the whites of the eyes.

What you need to know:
• Many problems cause red eyes and discharge; pinkeye is only one of them.
• It is very contagious.
• Pinkeye sometimes is known as conjunctivitis or a cold in the eye.

Get professional help if:
• Your child has irritated or swollen eyes and you are not sure of the cause. Typical causes: allergies, colds, chlorinated swimming pool water, dust, blocked tear ducts.
• Your child has recurrent eye irritations.

Supplies: prescribed antibiotics, paper towels.

Symptoms:
• red eyes
• discharge and mattering shut of eyes after sleep
• swelling of lids

What to check:
• Has your child had contact with someone with pinkeye?
• Can your child see normally?

Treatment:
• Home treatment should always be directed by your doctor. Different causes of pinkeye call for different therapies.
• Wash your hands after touching a child with pinkeye.
• Encourage frequent hand-washing.

• To protect other family members, have the sick child use paper towels or isolate his washcloth and towel.
• Discourage eye-rubbing.

PINWORM

Description: an infestation of the intestinal tract by small, parasitic worms.

What you need to know:
- Pinworms are the most common worms infesting children.
- Infected children may be highly irritated or unaware of the problem.
- The worms are only active at night.
- They are easily spread.

Get professional help if:
- You suspect your child has pinworms. Any itching around the anus, buttocks or vagina is sufficient cause to contact your doctor.

Supplies: penlight, prescribed worm medicine.

Symptoms:
- itching around the anus or buttocks, especially at night
- vaginal irritation

What to check:
- To see the worms, leave the child alone 1 to 2 hours after bedtime. Then examine anal area with a penlight.
- Pinworms are white, as thick as sewing thread, and very active.

Treatment:
- Your doctor will prescribe a worm medicine and program for its use.
- All family members should be treated at the same time.
- Strict family hygiene is part of the cure. Fingernails should be kept short and clean. All towels, linens, underclothes and bedclothes should be laundered.

PITYRIASIS ROSEA

Description: a rash that appears as a series of round or oval red patches.

What you need to know:	Get professional help if:
• This is a common, harmless rash that disappears on its own. • It typically lasts 3–8 weeks. • One attack confers immunity for life. • It is mildly contagious.	• You are not sure that a rash is pityriasis. It can be confused with other rashes, some of which are treatable.

Supplies: calamine lotion, OTC oral antihistamine.

Symptoms:	What to check:
• round or oval, salmon-pink patches that are slightly raised, have a crinkly surface and rim of fine scales • patches will not be tender but may itch mildly • primarily affects trunk, but may appear on limbs	• Is the rash symmetrical on the right and left sides of the body? If so, suspect pityriasis. • Did one, larger spot (called a "herald patch") appear a few days before the rash?

Treatment:
• No treatment is needed.
• Use calamine lotion or oral antihistamine to reduce the itching.
• Expose body to sunlight to hasten the departure of the rash.

Related topics: Ringworm.

PNEUMONIA

Description: an infection of the lungs.

What you need to know:
- Pneumonia is now rarely a serious infection.
- It has several different causes and can occur with greatly varying severity.
- Some forms are contagious while others are not.
- Common colds are *rarely* complicated by pneumonia.

Get professional help if:
- You suspect pneumonia. Your doctor will diagnose the cause of the infection and may prescribe treatment. Severely affected, chronically ill or very young children may need to be hospitalized.

Supplies: thermometer, prescribed antibiotics (for some pneumonias), expectorant cough medicine (for some pneumonias), aspirin (ASA)/acetaminophen (acet.).

Symptoms:
- cough
- fever*
- fast or difficult breathing
- stomach pain
- chest pain
- infants may flare nostrils and breathe noisily

What to check:
- Does your child suffer from asthma or cystic fibrosis? If so, pneumonia is more likely to strike and can be more serious.

Treatment:
- See your doctor. Pneumonia is actually several diseases with a common expression. Each case should be managed individually by a doctor.
- Give expectorant cough medicines if your doctor recommends them.
- Give ASA/acet. for fever.

Related topics: Asthma, Cystic Fibrosis.

*See Fever Guide, p. 27.

POISONING

Description: ingestion of medicine, cleaning products, petroleum-based products or other harmful substances.

What you need to know:
• Medicines, cleaners, house plants and other common items are the chief causes of poisoning.
• Safe storage can prevent poisoning, but be ready for emergencies with your local poison control center phone number.

Get professional help if:
• You suspect your child has swallowed or put into his mouth any harmful substance.

Supplies: syrup of ipecac, water, milk.

Symptoms:
• abdominal pain/diarrhea
• black-out/unconsciousness
• blurred vision/convulsions
• choking or trouble breathing
• confusion/drowsiness
• coughing up blood/nausea
• dizziness/behavior change
• rash/burn

What to check:
• Have any medicines, cleaners or other harmful substances been opened, or are any missing?
• Take container and sample of any vomit to hospital.

Treatment:
• Call the poison control center immediately.
• Do not induce vomiting unless you are told to do so. If you are told to, give 1 Tbsp. ipecac, followed by a glass of water.
• If help is not available, give 2-3 glasses of water or milk to dilute poison (only if child is conscious and can swallow). Take the child to a hospital.

Related topics: Breathing Emergency, Burn, Convulsion, Stomach Pain, Unconsciousness, Vision Problem, Vomiting.

POISON IVY

Description: a rash, often with swelling and blistering, caused by contact with poison ivy plants.

What you need to know:
- Poison ivy is one of the most common causes of rashes in children; the rash may last 2–3 weeks.
- Direct contact with plants is not necessary: clothing and pets can transmit the irritant.
- Children vary in sensitivity.

Get professional help if:
- Rash is extensive or severe. Small rashes respond to home treatment, but more serious outbreaks are best treated with prescribed oral steroids.

Supplies: towels, soap and water, fingernail clippers, Fels Naphtha, cleaning fluid, calamine lotion or prescribed antihistamines.

Symptoms:
- itchy rash, often in a line where plant brushed the child
- swelling
- reddening of the skin
- small or large blisters

What to check:
- Determine where child encountered poison ivy to prevent another contact.
- If the rash spreads after 4–7 days, the child has made new contacts.

Treatment:
- If itching is acute, lay a cold, wet towel on area and cover with a dry towel. Leave on for 30 minutes.
- Otherwise, bathe your child with soap and tepid water. Cut fingernails short to reduce temptation to scratch.
- Launder clothing with Fels Naphtha and clean shoes with cleaning fluid.
- Give prescribed antihistamines *or* calamine lotion to reduce the itching (don't combine the two).
- Teach your child to identify poison ivy leaves to avoid further trouble.

Related topics: Allergy, Blister, Hives.

POLIO

Description: a viral infection of the spinal cord that can cause paralysis or death.

What you need to know:
• Polio is entirely preventable with safe oral vaccines. *Get your child immunized.*
• Once the infection occurs, there is no cure.
• Most children who get polio show no symptoms.

Get professional help if:
• You suspect your child has polio. Diagnosis requires laboratory tests.
• Your child is not vaccinated and is exposed to polio.
• Your child is not yet vaccinated.

Supplies: aspirin (ASA)/acetaminophen (acet.).

Symptoms:
• headache
• loss of appetite
• vomiting
• neck pain
• nausea
• paralysis

What to check:
• Immunization records.
• Contact with known or suspected polio victims.

Treatment:
• Although there is no cure for polio, supportive treatment is available to make victims comfortable.
• Polio affects children with greatly varying severity. Treatment also varies.
• Give ASA/acet. to make your child more comfortable.

Related topics: Encephalitis, Meningitis.

RASH, NEWBORN

Description: common rash affecting newborns.

What you need to know:
- This is a very common rash, affecting 50% of all babies.
- It begins a few days after birth and disappears on its own within a week.

Get professional help if:
- None is needed.

Supplies: none.

Symptoms:
- raised red splotches on chest, back, face and extremities
- rash appears before infant is 5 days old

What to check:
- Is the rash possibly heat rash (see p. 131)? If so, it can be treated by making the baby's environment cooler and less humid, and by dressing him lightly.

Treatment:
- No treatment is necessary. The rash does no harm and goes away on its own.

REYE'S SYNDROME

Description: a serious illness, usually following influenza or chicken pox, that involves swelling of the brain.

What you need to know:
• Reye's syndrome is one of the least common causes of vomiting, but has received publicity because it can be life-threatening.
• An early diagnosis improves chances for total recovery.

Get professional help if:
• Your child develops symptoms of Reye's syndrome, especially if the child was given aspirin recently to ease symptoms of chicken pox or influenza. Call your doctor immediately.

Supplies: acetaminophen (acet.)—not aspirin (ASA).

Symptoms:
• vomiting, often severe
• confusion or lack of coordination

What to check:
• Has your child recently had chicken pox or influenza? Reye's syndrome strikes just when a child is recovering from one of these illnesses.

Treatment:
• Your doctor will decide what steps need to be taken to manage Reye's syndrome.
• Prevention is preferable to treatment. Doctors are not sure how Reye's syndrome occurs, but are now asking parents *not* to give aspirin to children with chicken pox or influenza. Acet. *is safe,* if given according to dosages on labels.

Related topics: Chicken Pox, Influenza, Vomiting.

RHEUMATIC FEVER

Description: a possible complication of strep throat that can cause permanent heart damage.

What you need to know:
• Prompt diagnosis and treatment of strep throat can prevent rheumatic fever.
• It can recur throughout life following strep infections.
• Half of all children who get rheumatic fever suffer heart damage.

Get professional help if:
• You suspect your child has strep throat (see p. 193).
• Your child develops the symptoms of rheumatic fever.

Supplies: thermometer.

Symptoms:
• arthritis (swollen, painful, inflamed joints)
• chest pain
• shortness of breath
• muscle-twitching
• rash on trunk and limbs
• fever*

What to check:
• Has your child had a throat infection several weeks prior to the appearance of the symptoms?

Treatment:
• Rheumatic fever must be treated by a physician. The disease is highly variable in its effects. Early treatment is always desirable.
• Prevention is far better than treatment for this disease. Report all sore throats to your doctor promptly so strep throat infections can be identified and treated early.

Related topics: Arthritis, Strep Throat.

*See Fever Guide, p. 27.

RINGWORM

Description: a skin infection caused by a fungus.

What you need to know:
- This common skin problem is painless and treatable.
- It mostly affects children.
- Ringworm fungus can be picked up through direct or indirect contact with infected persons or pets (not worms).

Get professional help if:
- You suspect ringworm but wish to have your diagnosis confirmed. It is not always easy to determine which skin rash a child has.
- Rash does not respond to treatment in several days.

Supplies: topical antifungal ointment (tolnaftate), griseofulvin (by prescription).

Symptoms:
- flat red spot that grows outward to assume a circular or horseshoe shape with a scaly rim and clearing center. Most common on face, arms, shoulders, groin (jock itch)
- scalp ringworm involves patchy hair loss, inflammation

What to check:
- Watch for spread of rash.

Treatment:
- Apply tolnaftate cream twice a day. Or if your doctor prescribes it, give griseofulvin orally.
- You should see some improvement within a week, though complete cure may take as long as 6 weeks.

Related topics: Athlete's Foot.

ROCKY MOUNTAIN SPOTTED FEVER

Description: a bacterial infection caused by the bite of a certain kind of tick.

What you need to know:
- Often, infection can be prevented by removing a tick soon after it attaches to the body.
- The disease can be cured with antibiotics, but can be fatal if untreated or treated too late.
- It is most common on the east coast, but also may occur in other areas.

Get professional help if:
- You see symptoms of this illness following a tick bite or after an outing when your child may have been bitten.
- You cannot detach a tick by following the steps described below.

Supplies: thermometer, alcohol, tweezers, petroleum jelly or oil, soap and water.

Symptoms:
- muscle pain
- unremitting fever*
- headache
- rash that starts on ankles and wrists, then spreads
- rash may turn into raised, purple-red spots
- difficulty breathing
- shock

What to check:
- Look for ticks promptly after outings to brushy or wooded areas. Ticks favor warm, moist spots on the body (behind ears, on scalp, under arms, near genitals).
- Try to identify the tick (save it if possible).

Treatment:
- First, put alcohol on the tick and surrounding skin. This may cause it to detach within a few minutes. If so, lift it off with tweezers.
- If alcohol doesn't work, apply petroleum jelly or thick oil (this may smother the tick and cause it to detach). Leave oil on 30 minutes.
- If the tick is still not detached, try to remove it with tweezers. Be sure to remove all parts of its body.
- Wash the area with soap and water; watch for signs of shock, breathing difficulty, fever.

*See Fever Guide, p. 27.

ROSEOLA

Description: a viral rash affecting young children and infants.

What you need to know:
• Roseola is a common disease in children of 6–12 months of age.
• There is no prevention or cure, but it goes away on its own.
• It is the only disease with a high fever *followed by* a rash. Fever lasts about 4 days.

Get professional help if:
• Your child seems severely affected.
• Symptoms of roseola are accompanied by coughing, vomiting or diarrhea.
• Fever lasts longer than 4 days.

Supplies: thermometer, aspirin (ASA)/acetaminophen (acet.), lukewarm water baths.

Symptoms:
• high fever (103°–105°F.)*
• rash, developing right after fever drops, with flat, distinct, red spots

What to check:
• Any high fever requires close observation. Diagnosis can only be confirmed when rash appears. By then, if it is *not* roseola, complications could have appeared.

Treatment:
• Treat the fever with ASA/acet. and lukewarm water baths as required.

• Watch your child closely for other symptoms.
• Permit moderate activity if your child feels like it; it does no harm.
• Your child is well when the rash disappears, in a day or two.

*See Fever Guide, p. 27.

SCABIES

Description: an infestation by a microscopic mite causing severe itching.

What you need to know:	**Get professional help if:**
• Scabies is becoming much more common. • It is spread by contact with infected individuals, or their clothing, bedding, towels, etc.	• You suspect scabies. Your doctor will prescribe an ointment or lotion and, when possible, oral antihistamine to reduce the itching.

Supplies: prescribed ointment or lotion, prescribed antihistamine.

Symptoms:	**What to check:**
• small pink bumps on the body • severe itching (worst right after bedtime), usually in webs between fingers or on wrists, hollows of elbows, nipples, navel, genitalia • until scratching obscures them, you might see dark ridges where mites burrowed	• Try to determine the source of the infestation.
Treatment: • Follow the instructions of your doctor. • Treat all family members at the same time. • Launder all clothing, linens and towels in hot water.	• See your doctor if the treatment seems to fail. Reinfestation is probably to blame.

SCARLET FEVER

Description: a variant form of strep throat, characterized by a red rash combined with other symptoms.

What you need to know:
• Scarlet fever (or scarletina) is no more serious than strep throat alone, and it can be cured with antibiotics.
• It is common and very contagious. One exposure does not confer immunity against recurrence.
• Complications, though rare, can be serious.

Get professional help if:
• You suspect your child has scarlet fever. It must be treated by a doctor.
• Even children with mild symptoms should be seen by your doctor with little delay.

Supplies: thermometer, prescribed antibiotic, aspirin (ASA)/acetaminophen (acet.), cold liquids, mild foods.

Symptoms:
• often begins with headache, vomiting, sore throat, fever*
• prickly, rough, red rash appears after a day or two over most of the body
• lymph glands in neck may become swollen

What to check:
• Rash is rough to the touch, like sandpaper. Also, the spots will go white temporarily if pressed with a finger.

Treatment:
• See your doctor for prescription of oral antibiotics or an injection.
• If given oral antibiotics, *be sure to administer the full 10-day course of pills.*
• Give ASA/acet. to ease fever.
• Offer cold liquids and mild foods to children with sore throats.
• Isolate the sick child until after he has been receiving antibiotics for 24 hours.

Related topics: Strep Throat, Tonsilitis.

*See Fever Guide, p. 27.

SCOLIOSIS

Description: a spinal defect, with many possible causes, leading to curvature of the spine.

What you need to know:
- Parents rarely notice this condition.
- Though it affects both sexes, it is most common in prepubescent girls.
- It is associated with periods of rapid growth.

Get professional help if:
- You suspect your child has scoliosis. It must be evaluated and treated by a doctor.
- *Prompt diagnosis is highly desirable.*

Supplies: none.

Symptoms:
- one shoulder blade is unusually high or prominent
- shoulders tilt
- posture makes one hip more prominent
- clothing that hangs unevenly

What to check:
- Ask whether your school system screens for scoliosis.
- Have your child bend over; check for curvature of the spine.

Curved spine

Treatment:
- Treatment for scoliosis is highly individual, and must be supervised by your doctor or a specialist.

SEVERED LIMB

Description: partial or complete separation of a limb from the rest of the body.

What you need to know:

• If a limb is completely severed, pack it in ice and a moist towel and take it with you for emergency treatment; reattachment is often possible.

• Stop bleeding by applying pressure to the artery that carries blood to the affected limb (see below).

• If pressure does not stop bleeding, apply a tourniquet. Do so *only* if there is no other way to save a child's life.

• Applying a tourniquet almost always guarantees the loss of the limb (see p. 43).

Get professional help if:

• A limb is severed. Your child's life may be in danger from loss of blood. The steps below will help slow blood flow while help comes.

Supplies: ice; towels; a strip of cloth at least 2 inches wide; a strong, short stick.

IF ARM IS SEVERED:

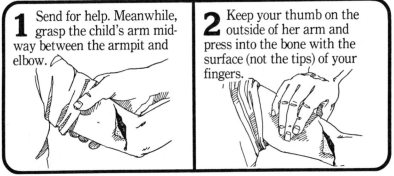

1 Send for help. Meanwhile, grasp the child's arm midway between the armpit and elbow.

2 Keep your thumb on the outside of her arm and press into the bone with the surface (not the tips) of your fingers.

(continued)

IF HAND IS SEVERED:

1 Send for help. Meanwhile, hold the child's hand palm up in your palm.

2 Press into her wrist bone with your thumb.

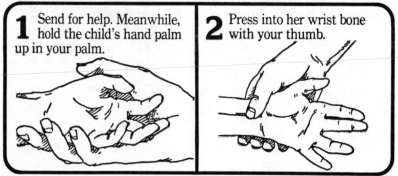

IF LEG OR FOOT IS SEVERED:

1 Send for help. Meanwhile, put the child on her back.

2 Place the heel of your hand on the front-center part of the groin (where the leg attaches to the trunk) and press into the pelvic bone.

3 Keep your arm straight for maximum strength. If this does not slow bleeding, cover the fingertips of one hand with the palm of your other hand and press down in the same manner as before.

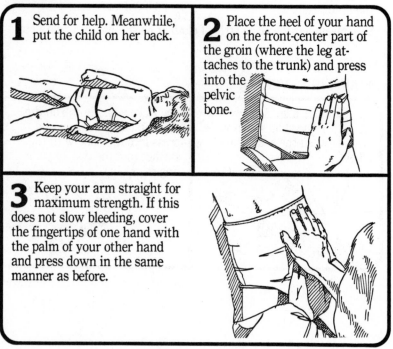

SHINGLES

Description: a rash, often with severe pain; caused by re-emergence of chicken pox virus.

What you need to know:	Get professional help if:
• It is rare in children under 10.	• Your child's symptoms are severe.
• It can be quite painful.	• Shingles affects your child's eye.
• It usually goes away in 1–2 weeks, sometimes longer.	

Supplies: aspirin (ASA)/acetaminophen (acet.), prescribed medications.

Symptoms:	What to check:
• rash preceded by intense itching, burning, pain	• Who in your household has not had chicken pox? While shingles itself is not contagious, a child with shingles can pass along the chicken pox virus to others.
• clustered red, raised spots that turn into teardrop blisters before breaking and forming scabs	
• rash may follow the line of nerves along the body	

Treatment:
• Isolate the child from other children with serious or chronic illnesses.
• Give ASA/acet. for discomfort.
• Your doctor may prescribe other medications.

Related topics: Chicken Pox.

SHOCK

Description: a dangerous drop in vital bodily functions, caused by intense pain, extreme fear, blood loss, overwhelming infection or other trauma.

What you need to know:
• Shock occurs in response to severe injuries or other medical emergencies. Treat the emergency *before* treating for shock.
• Always seek medical help as quickly as possible.

Get professional help if:
• You think your child is in shock. *Get help now.*
• It is rarely wise to move a shock victim to medical help. *Call for an ambulance.*

Supplies: blanket, pillow.

Symptoms:
• pale, moist, clammy skin
• weakness, apathy, incoherence, unresponsiveness
• rapid, weak pulse (check pulse at jawline)
• fast, shallow, irregular breathing/nausea

What to check:
• Deal first with the primary emergency that led to shock.

Treatment:
• Keep your child warm, not hot. Loosen tight clothing.
• Place her on her back; raise feet slightly with a pillow.
• Reassure her.
• Never administer fluids.
• *Never* move children who may have neck or spinal injuries.
• A child with face or mouth injuries may have trouble breathing. Place her on her side to ease breathing unless neck or spine are injured.

SINUSITIS

Description: an inflammation of the lining of the sinuses.

What you need to know:
• Sinusitis occurs in older children and has several causes.
• It often follows a cold.
• Sinusitis can be a side effect of many viral or bacterial infections.
• Sinusitis is usually brief, but can be chronic.

Get professional help if:
• Your child has a high fever* along with sinusitis.
• You detect pus-like discharge from one or both nostrils; this could indicate a foreign object in the nose.
• Your child's sinusitis is severe or chronic.

Supplies: thermometer, decongestants, nose drops, antihistamines as prescribed, aspirin (ASA)/acetaminophen (acet.), warm compresses, prescribed nose drops or antibiotics.

Symptoms:
• yellow, opaque or milky discharge from the nose
• headache
• other symptoms are usually caused by the allergy or infection that brought about the sinusitis

What to check:
• Be sure there is no foreign object in your child's nose.

Treatment:
• Try to relieve nasal stuffiness with decongestants, nose drops, or antihistamines as prescribed.
• Give ASA/acet. to relieve pain and fever.
• Apply warm compresses to painful areas.
• Your doctor may prescribe special nose drops or antibiotics.

Sinus cavities

Related topics: Cold, Hay Fever, Headache.

*See Fever Guide, p. 27.

SORE HEEL

Description: heel pain.

What you need to know:
- Children and adolescents commonly experience sore heels.
- About 90% of the time this is due to a blow on the heel or pounding the heels on the ground.

Get professional help if:
- Your child cannot rise on tip-toes. This may indicate a serious Achilles tendon problem.
- Sore heels are accompanied by fever* and swelling.
- Home treatment is not effective within six weeks.

Supplies: thermometer, 1/4-inch heel pads, aspirin (ASA)/acetaminophen (acet.).

Symptoms:
- pain in the heel, often centering on the heel bone

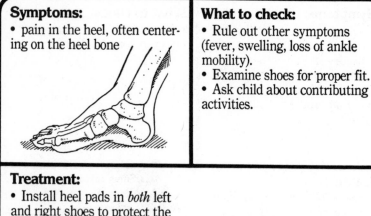

What to check:
- Rule out other symptoms (fever, swelling, loss of ankle mobility).
- Examine shoes for proper fit.
- Ask child about contributing activities.

Treatment:
- Install heel pads in *both* left and right shoes to protect the injured site and give it a chance to heal.
- Ask your child to restrict activities involving heavy jumping and running.
- Give ASA/acet. for discomfort.

Related topics: Bruise, Sore Muscle, Sprain.

*See Fever Guide, p. 27.

SORE MUSCLE (STRAIN)

Description: ache and pain in muscles, usually due to vigorous activity.

What you need to know:
• Muscle pain and strain are common in children and rarely a cause for concern.
• "Growing pains," muscle pains in lower legs, can awaken a child at night, but growth itself does not cause pain.

Get professional help if:
• Muscle pain persists, interfering with child's normal activities.
• You are concerned the pain might be in the joints.
• Muscle soreness is associated with a serious illness.
• Persistent limp appears.

Supplies: aspirin (ASA)/acetaminophen (acet.).

Symptoms:
• muscle soreness
• limping
• decreased flexibility or mobility.

What to check:
• Can your child's activities account for the soreness?
• Could the problem lie with the joints or ligaments and not with the muscles (see pp. 55, 190)?

Treatment:
• Give ASA/acet. to ease the pain.
• Allow your child to set his own level of activity. He'll probably curtail exercise, but if he feels like being active you can let him be.
• Urge your child to apply heat to the sore muscles by soaking in a hot tub.
• Give the sore muscles gentle massage to increase circulation.

Related topics: Arthritis, Leg Pain at Night, Sprain.

SORE THROAT

Description: throat pain, often in combination with other symptoms.

What you need to know:
• Most viral sore throats are harmless, but should be watched in case they are strep infections.
• Strep throat, a common illness, can have serious effects if untreated.
• Sore throats *not* caused by strep do not require antibiotics.

Get professional help if:
• Your child seems very ill, has a rash, or has trouble breathing. *Call your doctor immediately.*
• Your child has a high fever,* neck swelling, recent exposure to strep, or sore throat for more than 5 days.

Supplies: thermometer, aspirin (ASA)/acetaminophen (acet.), throat lozenges, honey, candy, warm salt water.

Symptoms:
• throat pain (must be inferred from behavior of infants, e.g., refusal of food)
• difficulty swallowing
• swollen glands
• fussiness

What to Check:
• Appearance of throat: is it inflamed?
• Are lymph nodes around the neck swollen?

Treatment:
• Ordinary sore throats can be relieved temporarily with ASA/acet.
• Honey, candy or throat lozenges will coat the throat and ease the pain temporarily
• Gargling with warm salt water makes some children feel better (a pinch of salt in a cup of water).

Related topics: Diphtheria, Mononucleosis, Strep Throat, Tonsilitis.

*See Fever Guide, p. 27.

SPLINTER

Description: a sliver of wood or other material embedded in the skin.

What you need to know:
• Slivers can be removed at home most of the time.
• Your main concern is to get out the whole splinter, and to do so without letting the injured area become infected.

Get professional help if:
• A splinter breaks off under the skin where it cannot be reached.
• A splinter wound is very deep or dirty and the last tetanus shot was more than 5 years ago.

Supplies: pin or needle, matches, alcohol, cotton, ice, tweezers, soap and water, adhesive bandage.

1 Sterilize a needle in a flame. Sterilize the area around the splinter with alcohol and cotton.

2 Numb the area with ice if it is very sore. Dig the splinter out with the needle, scraping gently to uncover.

3 For splinters that stick out, sterilize the tip of a pair of tweezers and pull the splinter out.

4 Wash the area with soap and water. Protect the area with an adhesive bandage.

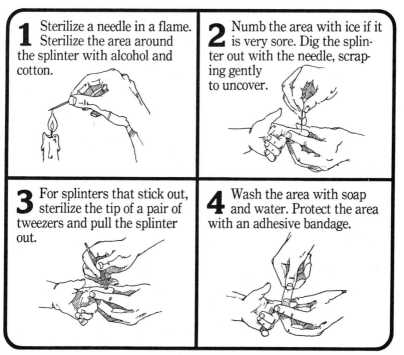

Related topics: Cut/Wound, Tetanus.

SPRAIN

Description: injuries of ligaments caused by overuse or improper use.

What you need to know:
- A sprain is a ligament injury at a joint. If the injury is not at a joint, it is probably a sore muscle (a "strain").
- Sprains, while common in older children, are not common in young children.

Get professional help if:
- The pain is extreme.
- A bone or joint is deformed or broken.
- The joint is too tender to be used 24 hours after the accident.
- There is significant swelling or loss of mobility.

Supplies: splint or elastic bandage, ice packs, heating pad, aspirin (ASA)/acetaminophen (acet.).

Symptoms:
- tenderness
- swelling
- loss of joint mobility

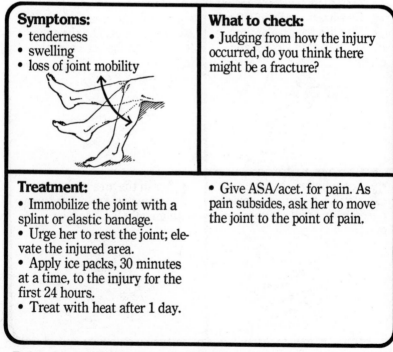

What to check:
- Judging from how the injury occurred, do you think there might be a fracture?

Treatment:
- Immobilize the joint with a splint or elastic bandage.
- Urge her to rest the joint; elevate the injured area.
- Apply ice packs, 30 minutes at a time, to the injury for the first 24 hours.
- Treat with heat after 1 day.
- Give ASA/acet. for pain. As pain subsides, ask her to move the joint to the point of pain.

Related topics: Broken Bone, Sore Muscle.

STOMACH FLU (GASTROENTERITIS)

Description: a viral infection of the stomach and intestines.

What you need to know:
• Some stomach flu is highly contagious, but is *not* influenza (see p. 144). Food poisoning is another, non-contagious form of gastroenteritis.
• Stomach flu may appear suddenly and last 1–7 days.
• Children under age 2 should be watched closely for dehydration (see p. 99).

Get professional help if:
• Your child shows signs of dehydration.
• Stomach pain is severe.
• Your child's stools are bloody or black.

Supplies: thermometer, clear liquids (juice, soda, Gatorade), selected foods, aspirin (ASA)/acetaminophen (acet.)

Symptoms:
• stomach cramps
• nausea/vomiting
• diarrhea
• fever*
• poor appetite

What to check:
• Watch for dehydration in small children, especially infants.
• Did several people get sick at the same time? It could be food poisoning.

Treatment:
• Treat fever, diarrhea and vomiting (see pp. 102, 115, 214).
• Wait for the infection to run its course.

Related topics: Diarrhea, Vomiting.

*See Fever Guide, p. 27.

STOMACH PAIN (ABDOMINAL PAIN)

Description: any pain in the abdominal region.

What you need to know:

• Stomach pain is a common complaint with many causes. The more acute and steady the pain, the more serious it is likely to be.
• Watch stomach pain very closely. Infants and toddlers may not be able to localize the pain.

Get professional help if:

• The pain persists longer than 4 hours.
• One specific spot is very tender to light pressure.
• You note bloody stools or greenish vomit.
• Your child simply looks very ill.

Supplies: thermometer, hot water bottle, acetaminophen (acet.)—*not* aspirin (ASA), clear liquids.

Symptoms:

• symptoms vary, depending on cause of the pain: vomiting, diarrhea, nausea and fever* are common
• in infants, legs drawn up and tensed

What to check:

• Look for specific pain centers, which might indicate appendicitis (see p. 54).
• Causes: new foods, milk products, gas, stress, constipation.

Treatment:

• Apply heat with a hot water bottle and monitor symptoms. Call your doctor if they persist for 4 hours or worsen.
• Don't give enemas or laxatives without the doctor's consent.
• Acet. (not ASA) may relieve pain.

• Offer her only clear liquids.

Related topics: Appendicitis, Constipation, Diarrhea, Stomach Flu, Vomiting.

*See Fever Guide, p. 27.

STREP THROAT

Description: a highly contagious throat infection caused by a bacterium called streptococcus.

What you need to know:
• Antibiotics will cure strep, but early diagnosis is helpful.
• If untreated, strep throat can have serious effects.
• When a child gets strep, his family and friends should be watched. The most common age is 5-14 years.

Get professional help if:
• Your child has a sore throat. You may be advised to bring your child in for a throat culture. Though sore throats are not emergencies that require immediate action, always call your doctor.

Supplies: thermometer, antibiotics, aspirin (ASA)/acetaminophen (acet.), throat lozenges, honey, candy, warm salt water (1 pinch of salt in a cup of water) for gargling.

Symptoms:
• sore throat
• red rash (sometimes)
• fever up to 104°F.*
• swollen lymph nodes
• vomiting
• abdominal pain
• headache centering over the eyes

What to check:
• Look for the rash (scarlet fever) that confirms a sore throat was caused by a strep bacterium.
• If your child has been exposed to strep, suspect a strep infection.

Treatment:
• Your doctor should direct the treatment of strep throat.
• It is *most important* to give your child *all* the antibiotics prescribed, even though the child seems well.
• Home treatment for strep, apart from the antibiotics, is like treatment of other sore throats. Give ASA/acet., lozenges, honey and candy to ease fever and soreness; encourage gargling.

Related topics: Mononucleosis, Rheumatic Fever, Scarlet Fever, Sore Throat, Tonsilitis.

*See Fever Guide, p. 27.

STYE

Description: a pimple-like abscess on the edge of the eyelid, caused by a bacterium.

What you need to know:
• Styes are usually minor nuisances that can be treated at home.

Get professional help if:
• The eyelid itself is swelling or your child's eyes become red or look infected.
• The stye resists home treatment after 3 days.

Supplies: warm compresses.

Symptoms:
• inflammation of upper or lower eyelid, often with a clearly formed pimple that may have a white center

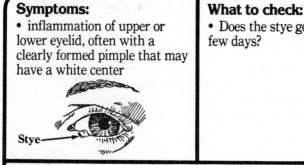

Stye

What to check:
• Does the stye go away in a few days?

Treatment:
• The object of treatment is to get the styes to open and drain.
• Apply warm compresses or cotton to the lids for 10–15 minutes, 3 or 4 times a day.

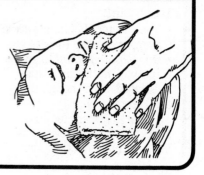

Related topics: Boil, Pinkeye.

SUDDEN INFANT DEATH (CRIB DEATH)

Description: the sudden death of an apparently normal, healthy infant for reasons that are unknown.

What you need to know:

• Death usually occurs during sleep, within seconds and without pain.

• Crib death is the leading cause of infant death after the first week of life; each year it strikes 10,000 babies.

• It is most common in infants between the ages of 1-6 months, and rarely occurs after 7 months.

• It occurs more often in winter than other seasons.

• Its cause is not known. Over the years, many explanations have been advanced, but none have been proven, and many have been disproven. It is *not* caused by choking, smothering, strangulation, enlargement of the thymus gland, pneumonia, injury of the spinal cord or allergy to cow's milk. Current thought is that it may be related to viral infection.

• Some infants have slight colds when they die, but there is no evidence that death is related to the cold.

• It occurs worldwide.

• Since there are no symptoms and the cause is unknown, it is impossible to predict or prevent SID. There is no indication that help is needed and no treatment that can be applied.

• Parents and siblings of infants who have died from crib death often feel severe guilt and depression. It is important for them to know the death was *not* due to neglect and is no one's fault—it cannot be prevented. Counseling and contact with other parents may be comforting and helpful; it can be obtained through:
National SIDS Foundation
Two Metro Plaza
8240 Professional Place
Suite 205
Landover, MD 20785
(301) 459-3388

• They will refer you to the chapter nearest you, or other organizations that may be of help.

SUNBURN

Description: skin burn, usually with redness but without blisters, caused by exposure to ultraviolet radiation.

What you need to know:
• Prevention is better than treatment. Products with PABA protect best.
• Don't expose infants to more than *15 minutes* of sun daily. Susceptibility varies; the fair-skinned, infants and young children are vulnerable.
• Reflected rays can burn; clouds don't filter burning rays.

Get professional help if:
• Sunburn causes dizziness, fever,* blisters, impaired vision or great pain.
• Exposure has been extreme. Medications taken *before* inflammation begins can reduce the severity of the burn.

Supplies: thermometer, cool compresses, baking soda and water, colloidal oatmeal, aspirin (ASA)/acetaminophen (acet.), prescribed ointments, lubricating creams.

Symptoms:
• pain
• redness

What to check:
• Have blisters appeared? They are evidence of a second-degree burn (rare), which requires a doctor's attention.

Treatment:
• Treat skin with cool compresses, a paste of baking soda and water, or colloidal oatmeal (use according to directions).
• Give ASA/acet. to reduce the pain, which is worst 6–48 hours after exposure.
• Apply prescribed ointments to ease the pain and promote healing.
• Apply lubricating creams only after the first day, as they may retain heat.
• Avoid OTC treatments with topical anesthetics; they prolong the healing time.

Related topics: Blister, Burn.

*See Fever Guide, p. 27.

SWALLOWED OBJECT

Description: swallowing any non-dissolving object.

What you need to know:
• Most objects pass through the body harmlessly. Unless you see signs of trouble, nothing more than careful watching is called for.
• Sharp, irregular objects are more likely to become lodged than smooth ones.

Get professional help if:
• Your child swallows a sharp object.
• Extended coughing, drooling or wheezing indicate breathing problems.
• Bloody stools, stomachache or vomiting indicate digestive tract problems.
• Your child points to where he feels the object lodged.

Supplies: crackers or dry bread, sieve made of window screen, warm water.

Symptoms:
• older children might report swallowing an object
• with younger children, often the disappearance of the object is the only sign that it has been swallowed

What to check:
• Is your child able to breathe normally? If not, see a doctor immediately. If your child can breathe, do not try to dislodge an object in his throat—let a doctor do so.

Treatment:
• If your child swallows a fish or chicken bone and it is lodged in his throat, give him a cracker or piece of dry bread. Swallowing these often clears the throat.
• If the object has passed into the stomach, it will probably pass on through the child's body.
• If the object is likely to become lodged, check your child's stools until the object has been passed.
• To check stools, break them up in a window screen sieve, washing them with warm water.

Related topics: Breathing Emergency, Choking, Cough.

SWIMMER'S EAR

Description: inflammation of the ear canal, common with children who swim frequently.

What you need to know:
• Frequent, sustained exposure of ear to water weakens the ear's protection against infection.
• Children prone to swimmer's ear should clean their outer ears with rubbing alcohol and cotton after swimming.

Get professional help if:
• Your child has swimmer's ear. Your doctor will prescribe a preparation to cure the inflammation and prevent it from spreading to the external ear.

Supplies: cotton, rubbing alcohol, petroleum jelly, prescribed antibiotics, aspirin (ASA)/acetaminophen (acet.).

Symptoms:
• discharge from ear
• ear pain worsened by pulling on the ear
• diminished hearing

What to check:
• To confirm diagnosis of swimmer's ear, press gently in on button in front of ear. If that hurts, your child probably has swimmer's ear.

Treatment:
• Keep ears dry until infection is cured. During baths cotton plugs coated with petroleum jelly will keep water out.
• Administer antibiotics as prescribed by your doctor.
• Give ASA/acet. for pain.
• Keep your child from swimming until the inflammation disappears.

Related topics: Earache, Hearing Loss.

SWOLLEN LYMPH GLAND

Description: enlargement of lymph gland in neck, groin or armpits, usually caused by infection.

What you need to know:
• Lymph glands are part of the body's defense against infection. When swollen and slightly tender, they are usually doing their job.
• The glands themselves can become infected and need treatment.

Supplies: thermometer.

Get professional help if:
• Glands are red and painful, as well as swollen.
• Glands remain swollen for more than 3 weeks. Soreness usually disappears in 2 days; swelling often lasts much longer.
• Earache or difficulty swallowing or breathing occurs.
• Your child seems generally ill.

Symptoms:
• swelling of the lymph glands
• may be tenderness, redness if glands are infected
• fever*

What to check:
• Check for cause of infection. Do not confuse swollen glands with mumps, which causes a swelling of the salivary glands. Mumps affects only glands lying behind, below and in front of earlobes.

Treatment:
• Normal swollen glands do not need to be treated.
• If you suspect your child has *infected* glands, see your doctor. He may prescribe antibiotics.

Related topics: Mononucleosis, Strep Throat, Tonsilitis.

*See Fever Guide, p. 27.

TEETHING

Description: tenderness of the gums of infants, caused by the eruption of teeth.

What you need to know:	Get professional help if:
• Not all babies teethe at the same time. Between 3 months and 3 years of age is typical. • Never let a child go to sleep with a bottle of milk or juice. Doing so increases the risk of tooth decay.	• Symptoms below are accompanied by signs of illness (fever,* loss of appetite, etc.). Otherwise, professional help is not needed for the eruption of teeth.

Supplies: thermometer, aspirin (ASA)/acetaminophen (acet.), teething rings, teething biscuits, ice wrapped in cloth.

Symptoms:	What to check:
• fussiness • drooling • chewing fingers or other objects • crying	• Consider other causes of symptoms: hunger, thirst, boredom, ear infection, a need for affection.

Treatment:
• Little can be done to help teething babies. Cuddling works as well as anything.
• Give ASA/acet. to relieve gum soreness.
• Try offering some children teething rings or biscuits, which help. Some teething babies like to chew cool objects (ice wrapped in cloth or a frozen teething ring).
• Avoid giving medications sold to relieve teething pain; they have not been proven to work.

*See Fever Guide, p. 27.

TESTICLE, TORSION OF

Description: the twisting of a testis, or part of a testis, that shuts it off from its blood supply.

What you need to know:
• This condition is not common.
• Prompt medical attention is critical if torsion occurs.

Get professional help if:
• Your boy has the symptoms of testicular torsion. Most testicular pain results from a blow to the groin, and disappears within an hour. Persistent abdominal or testicular pain is cause for concern.

Supplies: ice pack.

Symptoms:
• pain, usually intense, of the lower abdomen (undescended testis) or testis itself (if already descended)
• scrotum may be swollen, dark red
• nausea/vomiting

What to check:
• Is the pain the result of a blow? If you believe it is, treat the pain with an ice pack for an hour. Then, if the pain persists, call a doctor immediately.

Treatment:
• Torsion of a testicle must be treated by a physician as quickly as possible. There is no home treatment.

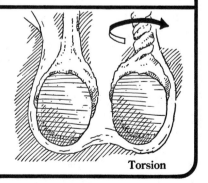

Torsion

Related topics: Hernia.

TESTICLE, UNDESCENDED

Description: failure of one or both testes to migrate from inside the body into the scrotum.

What you need to know:
• Though undescended at birth, often the testis migrates to the scrotum on its own.
• Surgery can usually correct an undescended testicle.
• Another condition, retractile testis, can be confused with undescended testis.

Get professional help if:
• Your child's scrotum does not appear normal. Your doctor will determine whether or not surgery will be required.

Supplies: none.

Symptoms:
• one or both testes are not present in the scrotum
• the scrotum itself may be small

Undescended testis

Normal testis

What to check:
• To distinguish from retractile testes, have your child pull his knees to his chest while sitting in a warm tub. This usually causes a retractile testis to descend.

Treatment:
• Confirmation of a diagnosis of undescended testicle, as well as its surgical cure, must be made by a physician.
• The surgery is best scheduled when a boy is 3-5 years old.

TETANUS

Description: a disease of the nervous system caused by bacteria entering the body through a cut.

What you need to know:
- With tetanus, prevention is the key: *get your child immunized.*
- Tetanus vaccinations must be given to each family member on a regular schedule.
- Deep wounds and wounds from objects encountered outdoors tend to cause tetanus.

Get professional help if:
- Your child needs tetanus immunization or needs a booster shot.
- Your child has a deep cut or wound and her immunization is not up to date.

Supplies: soap and water, antiseptic solution.

Symptoms:
- following a wound:
  - muscle stiffness, spasms
  - clenched jaw muscles
  - difficulty in swallowing
  - convulsions
  - difficulty breathing

What to check:
- Keep careful records on the immunization schedule for each family member.

Treatment:
- There is no home treatment for tetanus once it develops. Prevention (immunization and proper wound treatment) is the key.
- Cleanse wounds thoroughly and promptly, removing dirt and dead tissue. Treat with antiseptic solution.

- Get stitches for cuts and wounds that are long or widely opened.

Related topics: Bites, Animal and Human; Cut/Wound.

THRUSH

Description: a yeast infection of the mouth and tongue of young children.

What you need to know:	Get professional help if:
• Thrush causes no symptoms except white patches on the mouth and tongue. It may go away if ignored, but most parents want to treat it.	• Your child has thrush or you suspect he does.

Supplies: prescribed antibiotic.

Symptoms:	What to check:
• white patches on inside of cheeks, behind lips, or on tongue • patches look like dried milk, but will not wipe off with a clean handkerchief	• Are there blisters inside the mouth? If so, it might be canker sores, cold sores or herpes stomatitis.

Treatment:
• Apply prescribed antibiotic to patches as directed.

THYROID PROBLEM

Description: overproduction or underproduction of a hormone (thyroxin) by the thyroid gland.

What you need to know:
• Thyroid hormone affects metabolism and growth throughout the body.
• Thyroid production problems are treatable.
• Underproduction is difficult to detect in infants, but can lead to permanent problems.

Supplies: none.

Get professional help if:
• You detect signs of thyroid malfunction.

Symptoms:
• Underproduction:
-excessive drowsiness
-choking during nursing
-constipation
-slow growth
-thick, dry skin
-enlarged, protruding tongue

• Overproduction:
-nervousness/tremors
-weight loss/diarrhea
-abnormally moist, warm skin
-goiter
-trouble sleeping

Treatment:
• Diagnostic test can confirm that thyroid production is normal. These should be done routinely shortly after birth. Check with your doctor to confirm that this has been done for your child.
• Problems with thyroid production must be diagnosed and cured by a physician. Home treatment consists of noting the symptoms when they occur.

Related topics: Goiter, Hair Loss.

TIC

Description: jerky, spasmodic mannerisms of face or body that appear at times of stress and fatigue.

What you need to know:
- Tics are fairly common and are not indicative of serious nervous problems.
- When parents overreact to tics, they increase the stress that causes them.
- Tics often occur when child starts school, then subside.

Get professional help if:
- Voice tics and facial tics appear together. This might be Tourette's syndrome, which needs a doctor's attention.
- The tics don't seem to be decreasing and you are concerned.
- Tics seem to interfere with activities of everyday life.

Supplies: none.

Symptoms:
- twitching (usually of face muscles)
- blinking
- coughing
- jerking
- throat clearing

What to check:
- Squinting might be a tic, but it might also be caused by near-sightedness. Have your child's vision checked.

Treatment:
- Tics should be considered cosmetic problems, not nervous problems.
- Reassure your child, but do not pay great attention to tics.
- Try to identify and alleviate sources of stress in your child's life.
- Reduce fatigue or sources of allergens if they seem to contribute to the problem.

Related topics: Vision Problem.

TONSILITIS

Description: an inflammation and enlargement of the tonsils.

What you need to know:
• Tonsils are part of the lymph system and play a role in promoting health.
• Tonsils are normally large when children are 2-6; later they shrink.
• Doctors today question the benefits of tonsillectomies.

Get professional help if:
• Fever,* severe pain and difficulty in swallowing are also present. These may indicate abscessed tonsils.
• Your child has more than 5 attacks a year.

Supplies: thermometer, aspirin (ASA)/acetaminophen (acet.), throat lozenges, honey, candy, warm salt water, prescribed medication, penlight.

Symptoms:
• sore throat, with enlarged and sore tonsils (tonsilitis is not really an illness separate from other sore throats, but merely a sore throat that involves the tonsils)
• fever*

What to check:
• Use penlight to examine tonsils, throat.

Treatment:
• Home treatment for tonsilitis is identical to home treatment for colds or sore throats. The object is to make the child as comfortable as possible until the illness passes. Your doctor may order a throat culture and prescribe medication.

Related topics: Cold, Mononucleosis, Sore Throat, Strep Throat.

*See Fever Guide, p. 27.

TOOTHACHE

Description: tooth pain, usually caused by tooth decay.

What you need to know:
• Prompt attention to tooth pain is very important.
• Tooth decay is largely preventable through proper hygiene and exposure to stannous fluoride. If your water is not fluoridated, use fluoride tablets.

Get professional help if:
• You suspect your child has a toothache.
• Your child is due for a checkup. From the time he is 2 1/2-3 years old, he should get twice-yearly dental checkups.

Supplies: Popsicle stick or tongue depressor, aspirin (ASA)/aceteminophen (acet.), icepack.

Symptoms:
• pain, from slight twinges to constant throbbing
• the gum near the affected tooth may be red, swollen, and tender

What to check:
• Sometimes the signs of a toothache are obvious, but not always. If you suspect a toothache, tap gently on teeth with a Popsicle stick or tongue depressor. This causes no pain in healthy teeth.

Treatment:
• See your dentist as soon as possible.
• Use ASA/acet. and an icepack to reduce pain until your child can see the dentist.
• Contact a hospital emergency room in cases of severe pain.

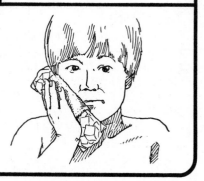

TUBERCULOSIS (TB)

Description: a contagious bacterial disease occurring in several forms.

What you need to know:
- Once common, TB is now rare, except in immigrant populations.
- Children under 2 years are much more vulnerable than older children.
- Children get TB from adults.
- A positive TB test may not mean that your child has it.

Supplies: thermometer.

Get professional help if:
- Your child has not been screened for TB (once a year up to 4 years, then every other year after that).
- Your child has been exposed to an adult infected with TB.
- Your child develops the symptoms of TB.

Symptoms:
- fever*
- loss of appetite/weight
- lack of energy
- cough
- loss of color
- irritability
- severe sweating in bed at night.

What to check:
- Since children get TB from adults (even adults with no symptoms), all adult family members of children with positive TB tests should also be tested. Other adults with frequent contact with the child should be tested as well.

Treatment:
- There is no home treatment for TB. Fortunately, the disease responds well to treatment with modern drugs. The key to avoiding this potentially serious disease is frequent TB screening.

- If you adopt a foreign-born child, make sure she has been screened for TB (this is almost always done routinely).

Related topics: Cough.

*See Fever Guide, p. 27.

UMBILICAL CORD INFECTION

Description: an infection of the cord and surrounding skin, before or after the cord has dropped off.

What you need to know:
• A slight amount of bleeding or oozing from the belly button scab is normal.
• Persistence of the oozing and the presence of red, irritated skin is not normal and should be checked.

Get professional help if:
• You believe the umbilical cord or surrounding skin are infected.

Supplies: rubbing alcohol, cotton swabs.

Symptoms:
• skin is red, irritated
• may be a smelly, oozing discharge

What to check:
• Look for signs of infection.
• Make sure his diaper is not covering the scab.

Treatment:
• If an infection has set in, it must be treated by your doctor. You can take preventive measures to hasten the healing of the scab left when the cord dries and drops off.
• Keep the scab dry and exposed to air. Fold diapers so that they do not cover the scab.

• Apply alcohol to the scab with a swab twice a day to keep it dry and clean.
• Swab scab with alcohol after baths.

UNCONSCIOUSNESS (FAINTING)

Description: a partial or total loss of consciousness, caused by reduced blood flow to the brain.

What you need to know:
- Symptoms of faintness: paleness, sweaty/clammy skin, dizziness, tingling in feet and hands, nausea/vomiting, blurred vision.
- Both serious and minor injuries and illnesses can cause fainting or unconsciousness.

Get professional help if:
- Your child loses consciousness and it is not due to breath-holding or pranks.
- Serious injury results as a child falls unconscious.
- Faintness occurs repeatedly.

Supplies: washcloth and cool water.

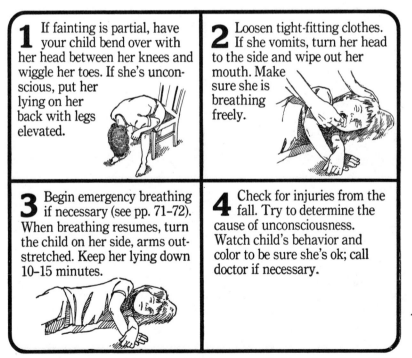

1 If fainting is partial, have your child bend over with her head between her knees and wiggle her toes. If she's unconscious, put her lying on her back with legs elevated.

2 Loosen tight-fitting clothes. If she vomits, turn her head to the side and wipe out her mouth. Make sure she is breathing freely.

3 Begin emergency breathing if necessary (see pp. 71–72). When breathing resumes, turn the child on her side, arms outstretched. Keep her lying down 10–15 minutes.

4 Check for injuries from the fall. Try to determine the cause of unconsciousness. Watch child's behavior and color to be sure she's ok; call doctor if necessary.

Related topics: Breath–holding, Cardiac Arrest, Choking, Convulsion, Dizziness, Electric Shock, Shock.

URINARY TRACT INFECTION

Description: an infection of the urinary system that can lead to a variety of problems.

What you need to know:
- Urinary tract infections can be tricky to detect and treat.
- They are far more common with girls than boys.
- With boys, they often are caused by a blockage, sometimes a serious problem.

Get professional help if:
- You detect any sign of urinary tract infection or blockage. Careful diagnosis and subsequent management is called for.

Supplies: thermometer, aspirin (ASA)/acetaminophen (acet.), juices, especially cranberry juice.

Symptoms:
- frequent, painful or bloody urination
- discharge
- foul-smelling urine
- bedwetting in a usually dry child
- abdominal or back pain
- fever*
- nausea

What to check:
- If your child has a fever over 101°F. or appears very ill, call your doctor immediately.

Treatment:
- Treatment must be managed by a physician.
- Until you see your doctor, give ASA/acet. for pain and administer large amounts of fluids. Cranberry juice has some antibacterial properties.

- Prevention of infections may involve training your daughter to wipe from front to back after using the toilet and not using bubble bath products.

Related topics: Backache, Bedwetting, Headache.

*See Fever Guide, p. 27.

VISION PROBLEM

Description: a short- or long-term impairment of vision.

What you need to know:
• Vision problems can be a sign of eye disease, another illness, or an injury.
• Difficulties with eyesight can be from a specific, correctable cause or might require treatment and/or eyeglasses.

Get professional help if:
• Any sign of a vision problem occurs.

Supplies: none.

Symptoms:
• eyes red, puffy, watery; eyelids red-rimmed, swollen
• eye rubbing, blinking, squinting, crossing
• dizziness, headaches, nausea, irritability after close work; complaints (blurred vision, "I can't see it.")

What to check:
• Is there a foreign object in eye?
• Is it an allergic reaction? Try to identify possible irritant.
• What specific situations cause the problem to occur?

Treatment:
• Consult your doctor or an ophthalmologist for any vision problems.

Related topics: Crossed Eyes, Eye Injury, Tic.

VOMITING

Description: expelling food from stomach through nose and mouth, a common symptom with many causes.

What you need to know:
- The most common cause of vomiting, by far, is a stomach viral infection.
- Infants often spit up, which is not vomiting.
- The main concern with vomiting is dehydration.

Get professional help if:
- Any vomiting does not stop within 12 hours or is combined with drowsiness, headache, abdominal pain, high fever*, labored breathing.
- Vomited material is yellow or green more than once or twice.
- Vomiting develops after child seems recovered from chicken pox or influenza (see p. 191).

Supplies: thermometer; ice chips; cool, clear liquids, light foods (Jello, broth, apple juice, Popsicles), flat carbonated beverages.

Symptoms:

What to check:
- Look for signs of dehydration: listlessness, dry mouth, sunken eyes, crying without tears, infrequent urination.

Treatment:
- Watch infants under 5 months closely and call your doctor. Withhold milk.
- Wait until 2 hours have passed without vomiting, then offer ice chips (but not to babies). Then ease cool liquids in with frequent small amounts (1 tsp.–1 Tbsp. at 10-minute intervals).
- Increase clear liquids gradually.
- Do *not* feed chicken broth, which contains fat and may be difficult to digest.
- Keep the child on clear liquids for a day. Then allow light food (Jello, applesauce, dry toast, rice, bananas), then regular food.

Related topics: Reye's Syndrome, Stomach Flu, Strep Throat.

*See Fever Guide, p. 27.

WART

Description: benign tumors of the outer layer of skin, caused by a virus.

What you need to know:
- About 65% of warts disappear on their own within 2 years.
- Warts rarely cause any pain or trouble, while medical measures to remove them can lead to more problems than the warts themselves.

Get professional help if:
- Warts are painful or located somewhere (as on eyelid) where treating them at home would be difficult.
- Warts interfere with proper nail growth.

Supplies: OTC preparation for removing warts.

Symptoms:
- skin-colored bumps, most often found on hands but also on feet (plantar wart) or almost anywhere else

What to check:
- To distinguish between calluses and warts, check to see whether the bump interrupts the natural line of the skin. If so, it is a wart. Calluses often form over warts.

Treatment:
- The best treatment is to ignore the wart. It will probably go away on its own.
- Painful or objectionable warts can often be removed with commercial preparations sold in pharmacies.

WHOOPING COUGH (PERTUSSIS)

Description: a serious respiratory infection that causes severe coughing spasms.

What you need to know:
• If untreated, whooping cough can lead to death, especially in very young children. *Get your child immunized.*
• Modern treatment brings most children through the illness with no aftereffects.

Get professional help if:
• Your child has not been immunized with DPT vaccine.
• Your child develops symptoms of whooping cough.
• Your child has been exposed to whooping cough.
• Your child has a cough that worsens after 2 weeks.

Supplies: thermometer, prescribed medications.

Symptoms:
• spasms of coughing, punctuated by whooping gasps for breath, ending with vomiting
• cough worsens over a long period of time
• low (100–101°F.) fever* preceding the coughing phase of the illness

What to check:
• Be sure your infant is immunized. Infants are *not* born with protection against whooping cough. They are at risk until immunized.

Treatment:
• Your doctor will supervise the management of whooping cough. With antibiotics, injections of antibodies, and good care, most children with whooping cough do well.

Related topics: Cough, Croup, Epiglottitis.

*See Fever Guide, p. 27.

Part 4

Appendix

GUIDE TO RESOURCES

BOOKS

Pregnancy and Childbirth

Borg, Susan and Lasker, Judith. *When Pregnancy Fails* (Beacon).
Donovan, Bonnie. *Cesarean Birth Experience* (Beacon).
Hotchner, Tracy. *Pregnancy and Childbirth: The Complete Guide for a New Life* (Avon).
Kitzinger, Sheila. *The Complete Book of Pregnancy and Childbirth* (Knopf).

Child Development

Brazelton, T. Berry. *Infants and Mothers* (Dell).
—. *Toddlers and Parents* (Delacorte).
Caplan, Frank. *The First 12 Months of Life* (Grosset and Dunlap).
—. *The Second 12 Months of Life* (Grosset and Dunlap).
Leach, Penelope. *Your Baby and Child, From Birth to Age Five* (Knopf).

Parenting

Acus, Leah Kunkle. *Quarreling Kids: Stop the Fighting and Develop Loving Relationships Within the Family* (Prentice Hall).
Colman, Arthur and Libby. *Earth Father/Sky Father: The Changing Concept of Fathering* (Prentice Hall).
Gregg, Elizabeth, ed. *What to Do When There's Nothing to Do* (Avon).
Kelly, Marguerite and Parsons, Elia S. *Mother's Almanac* (Doubleday).
Knight, Bryon. *Enjoying Single Parenthood* (Van Nostrand Rinehart).
Lansky, Vicki. *Practical Parenting Tips* (Meadowbrook Press).
—. *Dear Babysitter* (Meadowbrook Press).
Lerman, Saf. *Parent Awareness* (Winston).
Sullivan, S. Adams. *Father's Almanac* (Doubleday).

Food and Nutrition

Goldbeck, Niki and David. *The Supermarket Handbook* (New American Library).
Lansky, Vicki. *Feed Me, I'm Yours* (Meadowbrook Press).
—. *The Taming of the C.A.N.D.Y. Monster* (Meadowbrook Press).
La Leche League. *The Womanly Art of Breastfeeding* (La Leche League).

MAGAZINES AND NEWSLETTERS

American Baby, 575 Lexington Ave., New York, NY 10022, (212) 752-0775. Monthly; for expecting parents through those of one-year-olds.

Baby Talk, 185 Madison Ave., New York, NY 10016, (212) 679-4400. Monthly; for expecting parents through those of two-year-olds.

Growing Child, 22 N. Second St., Lafayette, IN 47902, (317) 423-2624. Monthly; for parents of newborns through those of six-year-olds.

Mothers Today, 441 Lexington Ave., New York, NY 10017, (212) 867-4820. Bimonthly; for expecting parents through parents of four-year-olds.

Mothering, Box 2208, Albuquerque, NM 87103, (505) 867-3110. Quarterly; for parents of newborns through those of five-year olds, though some articles cover older children.

Parents Magazine, 685 Third Ave., New York, NY 10017, (212) 878-8700. Monthly; for expecting parents through those of pre-teenagers.

Pediatrics for Parents, 176 Mount Hope Ave., Bangor, ME 04401, (207) 942-6212. Monthly; for expecting parents through those of teenagers.

Practical Parenting Newsletter, 18326A Minnetonka Blvd., Deephaven, MN 55391, (612) 475-1505. Bimonthly; for expecting parents through those of grade-schoolers.

Working Mother, 230 Park Ave., New York, NY 10169, (212) 551-9412. Monthly; for parents of infants through pre-schoolers.

RESOURCE GROUPS

American Academy of Pediatrics, Office of Public Education, 1801 Hinman Ave., Evanston, IL 60204; (312) 869-4255. Free list of publications on such topics as car seats, infectious diseases, accidents, child abuse, day care, drugs, nutrition, handicaps, genetic screening.

American Red Cross. Contact your local chapter to get information on the many courses and pamphlets available. Not all programs are available through all chapters. Some of the courses offered include first aid, family health and home nursing, swimming, parenting and C.P.R. (cardiopulmonary resuscitation).

Department of Health and Welfare, Poison Control Product Information Section, Laboratory Center for Disease Control, LCDC Building, Tunney's Pasture, Ottawa, Ontario K1A OL2, Canada; (613) 992-0979.

International Childbirth Education Association, P.O. Box 20048, Minneapolis, MN 55420; (612) 854-8660. Local services include childbirth education classes; health-care referrals on request. Free publications list.

La Leche League International, 9616 Minneapolis Avenue, Franklin Park, IL 60131, (312) 455-7730. Self-help organization for mothers, encouraging breast-feeding. Local weekly meetings; trained counselors can also answer questions by phone. Free publications list available upon request.

National Committee for the Prevention of Child Abuse, P.O. Box 2866, Chicago, IL 60690; (312) 663-3520. Provides informational packets on child abuse.

National Genetics Foundation, Inc., 555 West 57th Street, NY 10019; (212) 586-5800. Directs people in need of genetic services to them. Provides and reviews questionnaires on family health history. Free publications list.

National Institute of Mental Health, 5600 Fishers Lane, Parklawn Building, Room 15C17, Rockville, MD 20857; (301) 443-4515. Answers requests for mental health information for the public. Pamphlets and single free copies of publications on children's mental health, autism, and depression are available.

National Poison Center Network, 125 Desoto Street, Pittsburgh, PA 15213; (412) 647-5600. Offers home poison control materials. Sheet of 12 Mr. Yuk stickers, $1. Home poison prevention education kit and poison plant list, a list of 50 possibly toxic indoor and outdoor plants, available for nominal fees.

Parents Anonymous (P.A.) Hotline: in California, (800) 352-0386; outside California, (800) 421-0353. Offers on-the-spot counseling and a price list of nine items (booklets, pamphlets, etc.) parents can get to help prevent child abuse.

Parents Campaign for Handicapped Children and Youth, 1201 16th Street NW, Washington, D.C. 20036; (202) 822-7900. Booklet available for $2.00.

Parents Without Partners, Inc., 7910 Woodmont Avenue, Bethesda, MD 20814; (301) 654-8850. Provides support through family educational and adult activity programs conducted by local volunteers. Information on seminars, community workshops, support groups, and publications for single parents available upon request.

Physicians for Automotive Safety, P.O. Box 208, Rye, NY 10580; (914) 253-9525. Publishes a pamphlet, available for 50¢, that describes recommended car seats and other safety restraints for infants and children. Includes names and descriptions of crash-tested infant carriers and infant/toddler seats currently on the market.

U.S. Consumer Product Safety Commission, Washington, DC 20207; (800) 638-2772. Provides information on the safety and effectiveness of various products.

GLOSSARY

Italicized words are also defined separately.

A

abdomen the area of the body just below the diaphragm, containing the stomach, intestines and many other organs.

abscess an infected area filled with pus and surrounded by inflammation.

acet. an abbreviation for *acetaminophen.*

acetaminophen (acet.) a drug commonly substituted for *aspirin,* coming in both liquid and tablet form.

acid burn a burn caused by acid, such as muriatic acid or battery acid.

acute refers to suddenly appearing or severe conditions. Opposite of *chronic.*

alkali burn a burn caused by a base, such as sodium hydroxide (used in drain cleaners and oven cleaners).

allergen a substance that causes an *allergic reaction.*

allergic reaction an inflammatory bodily response to contact with some object that does not bother most people. Common allergic reactions include sneezing, watery or itchy eyes, nasal congestion and hives.*

anesthesia the loss of sensation, usually caused by drugs administered to counter the pain of medical procedures.

antibacterial ointment a salve or ointment that contains agents to kill bacteria that might start an *infection.*

antibiotic a drug that kills certain bacteria, but not *viruses.*

antihistamine a class of drugs that suppresses the *allergic reaction.*

anti-nauseant a class of drugs that suppress the *nausea* that can accompany motion sickness.*

antitoxin a substance produced in the blood to fight a specific *poison* (toxin). Antitoxins are produced by the human body, but some can be created artificially by infecting animals so that they create antitoxins, which are then purified for injection into humans.

anus the opening at the end of the *rectum.*

ASA an abbreviation for *a*cetylsali-cylic *a*cid or *aspirin.*

aspirin a drug commonly given to relieve headache,* sore muscles,* sore throat,* or to reduce fever.* It comes in tablet, gum and suppository form.

B

bacitracin an *antibiotic* commonly contained in *antibacterial ointments.*

bacterial infection an *infection* caused by one of many possible bacteria (tiny one-celled organisms). Unlike *viral infections,* bacterial infections respond to *antibiotics.*

benign refers to *tumors* that are not spreading to other body tissues. Opposite of *malignant.*

bronchioles the smallest air passages in the lungs.

C

cardiogram the printed results of a cardiograph or EKG, an instrument used to record movements of the heart.

chlorpheniramine an *antihistamine.*

chronic refers to an illness or symptom that is persistent and long-lasting, as opposed to *acute.*

ColdHot Pack a commercial product that is capable of being heated or chilled for use as a *compress.*

coma the condition of unconsciousness,* especially prolonged unconsciousness.

compress a cloth or container used to apply heat or cold to the body.

conjunctivitis an inflammation of the membrane that lines the eye socket or inner surface of the lids. A common form is called "pinkeye."*

*See main entry.

constricting band an encircling band of cloth or rope that is used to restrict the flow of blood from a wound. The term is often used instead of *"tourniquet"* because too many people believe a tourniquet is supposed to cut off the flow of blood completely.

contagious refers to an illness that can be passed from one person to another.

convalescence a period of rest and gradual return to health and strength after an illness.

CPR course a course in the techniques of CPR (cardio*p*ulmonary *r*esuscitation), used to revive people whose breathing or heartbeats have stopped.

cutaneous larvae migrans the microscopic larvae of hookworms. Can cause creeping eruption.*

D

defecate the act of moving the bowels.

delirium an altered state of consciousness during which disorientation (e.g., not recognizing people) and hallucinations (seeing or hearing things) may occur.

DPT immunization a vaccination giving protection against *d*iptheria,* *p*ertussis (whooping cough)* and *t*etanus.*

Dramamine a trade name for a common *anti-nauseant* drug.

E

elixir a sweetened mixture of alcohol and water, used as the base for many medicines.

enema the injection of a liquid into the *rectum* to cause one to *defecate.*

enzyme a chemical in the body that aids in certain chemical reactions, such as the breakdown of food into nutrients.

epiglottis a flap of tissue at the top of the trachea (windpipe) that closes it off when food or drink is swallowed.

Eustachian tubes the tubes leading from the rear of the nose and throat to each ear.

expectorant a medicine designed to break up or liquify congested secretions in the lungs, making it easier for the lungs to be cleared by coughing.*

F

febrile refers to fever* or a feverish state.

febrile seizure a condition involving uncontrolled movements of limbs or general shaking (convulsion*) caused by a high fever.*

flu a short name for influenza*

folic acid a *vitamin* that promotes healthy blood function.

fungus a family of germs that may cause *infections,* most often skin infections.

G

gamma globulin the part of the blood that carries the antibodies that fight diseases. It is sometimes taken from a person who has developed antibodies for a specific disease and injected into someone who is ill with that disease.

gastric bleeding a condition in which there is bleeding from the stomach walls.

generic a word applied to drugs sold under a descriptive or chemical name rather than a brand name. Generic drugs usually cost less than brand-name drugs.

genetic refers to tendencies or physical characteristics acquired by inheritance, through the genes. Susceptibility to some illnesses is related to a person's genetic inheritance.

germ a word used loosely instead of virus or bacterium to indicate the cause of disease or *infection.*

glomerulonephritis a specific kind of kidney inflammation.

glucagon a hormone produced in the pancreas. Glucagon breaks down glycogen (sugar) in the liver so it can enter the blood stream and increase the amount of sugar available to cells. Sometimes used to treat diabetes.*

*See main entry.

220

groin the part of the body where the thighs join the trunk; the site of the genitals.

H

heart palpitations an irregularly rapid beating of the heart.

hemangiomas a type of birthmark* caused by a cluster of small capillaries under the skin. Common hemangiomas are "stork bites" or salmon patches and strawberry marks.

hematocrit the percentage of the space in whole blood that is occupied by red blood cells. Recorded as part of most blood tests.

hemoglobin the part of the blood that carries oxygen. Recorded as part of most blood tests.

hereditary refers to traits or characteristics passed along genetically at the moment of conception.

herpes viruses a group of 3 *viruses*. Herpes simplex 1 causes cold sores* and canker sores.* Herpes simplex 2 causes venereal disease. Herpes zoster causes chicken pox* and shingles.*

hydrocortisone cream an ointment containing a hormone (often called cortisone) that reduces the severity of some symptoms.

I

immobilize to render some body part stationary; a splint, for example, secures a broken bone* in a fixed position, immobilizing it.

immunization a procedure in which a weakened form of a disease-causing agent is introduced into the body, provoking the body to build up an immunity to that disease.

incubation refers to the time between exposure to a disease and expression of the symptoms of that disease.

ineffective cough refers to a "dry" cough* that does not bring up any liquid from the respiratory system. Also called a non-productive cough.

infection condition caused by *viruses*, bacteria or parasites that may produce redness, swelling or fever.* Local infections affect only a small part of the body (e.g., an infected cut); general infections affect the body as a whole (e.g., a cold*). Untreated local infections can become general.

inflammation a symptom of *infection* or injury that usually involves redness, swelling and pain. The "-itis" at the end of many disease names often means "inflammation of." Hence bronchitis* is an inflammation of the bronchial tubes, tonsilitis* an inflammation of the *tonsils*, and so on.

intermittent refers to a pain or some other symptom that comes and goes rather than persisting.

insulin a hormone secreted by the pancreas that allows body cells to use blood sugar for energy.

J

jaundice a symptom characterized by yellowish skin and a yellow tint in the whites of the eyes. Common in newborns and associated with liver and blood dysfunction.

jock itch a skin *infection* of the *groin* caused by a *fungus*.

joint a location on the body that hinges, rotates or pivots to allow flexibility and movement (e.g., at the knee, in the shoulder, in the jaw, in the spine).

K

kidney dialysis a process by which impurities are removed from the blood by a machine when the kidneys cannot perform that function.

*See main entry.

221

L

lesion refers broadly to a localized unhealthy condition, such as a sore on the skin or scar on the lung.

lethargy a state of reduced vigor and consciousness, a general feeling of weakness and indifference.

ligament a connecting strand of tissue that ties bones together at a *joint* or attaches a *muscle* to a bone.

lymphangitis a technical word for blood poisoning.*

lymph nodes the enlarged sections of the channels that carry lymphatic fluid. They can become tender and enlarged in response to some illnesses, a condition often called "swollen lymph glands."*

Lytren a solution of water, minerals and sugar, designed to combat dehydration.*

M

malady a general term for a disorder or illness.

malaise an overall sense of not feeling well.

malignant a condition or growth that may spread if left untreated. It may or may not be cancerous. Opposite of *benign*.

Maltsupex a substance that can be added to an infant's formula to soften the stools in case of constipation.*

metabolic condition a condition affecting the overall chemical activities of cells.

metabolism the many complex chemical processes by which cells utilize oxygen, break down food, build tissue and discard waste.

N

nasal aspirator a squeeze-ball device for removing fluids from the nasal passages.

nausea the feeling that one may vomit.

nurse practitioner a nurse with graduate training (usually one or two years beyond the nursing degree) who has skills in history-taking, physical examination and care of many minor illnesses.

O

ophthalmologist a doctor who specializes in eye problems.

oral steroids a class of hormones in the cortisone family that can be taken by mouth.

orthopedic services the medical treatment of the skeletal system, including surgery or physical therapy.

P

palate the roof of the mouth, comprised of a hard and a soft part. The soft part is important in speech.

paramedical personnel people with various levels of medical training, but without a medical degree.

patient advocate an employee of a clinic or hospital whose responsibility is to act officially on behalf of patients in matters of medical education, treatment and other patient concerns.

Pedialyte a solution of water, minerals (such as salt) and sugar that can be given by mouth (usually with a bottle) in case of dehydration.*

pedodontist a dentist who specializes in the treatment of children.

placenta the organ that develops in the womb between the embryo and the wall of the uterus. Its functions are to pass oxygen and nutrients to the fetus and to remove waste materials.

plantar wart a type of wart* that occurs on the sole of the foot.

poison any substance which, if breathed or taken in the mouth can produce toxic effects. Thousands of household items, from *aspirin* to crayons to houseplants to perfume to plaster, can be poisonous to children.

postnasal drip the drainage of mucus from the nasal passages into the throat.

prepubescent refers to a child who has not reached *puberty*.

preventive health care a variety of measures designed to prevent medical problems. Includes such steps as *immunization* and dental checkups.

*See main entry.

protracted vomiting a period of vomiting* that lasts longer than 6 to 12 hours.

puberty the time at which adult sexual characteristics begin to develop in children.

R

rabies a *viral infection* affecting mammals, including man. Usually acquired after being bitten by a rabid animal.

rectum the lower part of the lower intestine, ending at the *anus.*

retractile testis a *testicle* that, having once been in its proper place in the *scrotal sac,* has temporarily withdrawn back into the lower *abdomen.*

S

salivary glands the glands located in the area where the jaw meets the neck. These glands secrete saliva.

scrotal sac the external sac that contains the *testicles (testes).*

seizure a convulsion* or series of convulsions, involving uncontrollable and often violent muscle *spasms.*

sepsis an *infection* in which bacteria circulate in the bloodstream.

sickle-cell anemia a type of anemia,*a blood disorder resulting in abnormally low *hemoglobin.* Especially prevalent among American Blacks.

silver nitrate a chemical compound routinely applied to the eyes of newborns to protect them against eye *infection* with gonococcus bacteria (gonorrhea). Such *infections* often impair vision.

spasm a sudden, involuntary contraction of a *muscle* or group of muscles.

sputum the mucus that is brought up by coughing.*

staphylococcus a family of bacteria, including several bacteria that can cause *infections* (called staph infections).

suppository a medication designed to be given by insertion into the *rectum* or vagina.

suppressant a medication intended to stop or limit certain symptoms, usually coughing.*

symptom a malfunction of the body or a part of the body resulting from disease.

syrup of ipecac a drug that induces vomiting;* to be used as directed by a doctor or poison control center after ingestion of certain *poisons.*

T

tepid refers to lukewarm temperature, not hot and not cold.

testicle (plural: testes) one of the male reproductive organs. It produces sperm and male hormones.

thymus gland a gland in the upper chest; thought to be disease-fighting.

tolnaftate an antifungal drug.

tonsillectomy an operation to remove the *tonsils.*

tonsils a pair of protective structures at the back of the throat that can fight *infection,* but that sometimes get infected themselves.

topical anesthetic an anesthetic (drug that reduces sensation, including pain) that is applied externally to the skin.

torso the trunk of the body.

Tourette's syndrome a *genetic* condition characterized by uncontrollable muscle *spasms* and vocalizations.

tourniquet a tight band around an arm or leg, used to stop bleeding that won't stop with local pressure.

tracheotomy an emergency medical procedure in which the trachea (windpipe) is cut, usually so a tube can be inserted to permit a choking* victim to breathe.

tremor an involuntary shaking or vibration of a *muscle* or limb.

tumor a swelling or enlargement of a body part, not necessarily malignant.

*See main entry.

223

U

ulcer an open, inflamed *lesion* of the skin or other tissue. Often refers to peptic ulcers of the stomach lining, although there are many other types of ulcers.

ultraviolet radiation a type of radiation, usually associated with sunlight. Ultraviolet rays cause tanning and sunburn.*

umbilical cord the tube-like cord that connects a fetus to the *placenta,* supplying nutrition and removing wastes. It is cut at birth and eventually withers and falls off, leaving the navel.

unremitting fever a fever* that remains high with no relief. The opposite of *intermittent.*

V

venom a *poison* (toxin) secreted by an animal or insect.

vertebrae the 25 bones that form the spine, encircling the spinal cord.

viral infection an *infection* caused by a virus, as opposed to a *bacterial infection.* Viral infections generally resist the *antibiotics* that kill bacteria, and most disappear when they have run their course.

virus a *germ* that must live inside body cells to multiply.

vitamin a chemical that the body itself cannot manufacture. Involved in body *metabolism.*

vitamin B_{12} a *B-complex vitamin* helpful in preventing anemia.*

Y

yeast infection an *infection* caused by a bacterium called monila. Common examples are thrush,* certain diaper rashes* and (in adolescent females) vaginal infections.

*See main entry.

INDEX

Boldface numbers refer to step-by-step entries. See the Glossary (p. 219) for definitions of key terms. See the Symptoms Index (p. 49) for specific symptoms.

A

Accident prevention, 17, 20-21
Acne, **51**
Allergy, **52**, 56, 62, 74, 75, 86, 92, 96, 108, 126, 138, 165, 170, 185, 206
Anatomy
  infants and children, 44-45
Anemia, **53**, 104, 150, 161
Appendicitis, **54**, 192
Appetite, loss of, 133, 135, 141, 156, 159, 160, 171, 191, 200, 209
Arthritis, **55**, 121, 137, 147, 174, 187
Artificial respiration
  see Breathing emergency, Cardio-pulmonary Resuscitation.
Aspirin, acetaminophen
  for fever, 27-29
  recommended doses, 30-31
  see also individual step-by-step entries.
Asthma, 52, **56**, 74, 75, 82, 92, 96, 98, 108, 126, 144, 168
Athlete's Foot, **57**, 66, 175

B

Backache, **58**, 59, 212
Back or neck injury, 58, **59**, 73
Bandages, 41, **43**, 73
Bedwetting, **60**, 100, 212
Birthmark, **61**, 154
Bites
  animal and human, **63**, 203
  insect, **62**, 138
  poisonous snake, **64-65**
Blister, 57, **66**, 67, 68, 77, 83, 119, 125, 131, 135, 143, 170, 183, 196, 204
  see also Cold sore.
Blood poisoning, **67**, 68, 94, 97
Boil, 67, **68**, 194
  see also Gum boil.

Breast enlargement, **69**
Breath-holding, **70**, 91, 104, 211
Breathing
  difficulty, 52, 53, 56, 74, 75, 86, 96, 98, 111, 140, 148, 162, 168, 169, 174, 176, 184, 197, 199, 203, 214, 216
  emergency, **71-72**, 79-80, 83, 84-85, 96, 98, 105, 109, 169, 197, 211
Broken bone, **73**, 76, 190
Bronchiolitis, 52, 56, **74**, 75, 82, 86, 98
Bronchitis, 52, 74, **75**, 82, 86, 92, 96, 98
Bruise, 73, **76**, 89, 150
  to eye, 113
  to fingernail/tip, 117
  to heel, 186
Burn, 21, 66, **77**, 109, 169
  chemical, of eye, 113
  see also Sunburn.

C

Canker sore, **78**, 204
Cardiac arrest, 71-72, **79-81**, 84-85, 105, 109, 211
Cardiopulmonary Resuscitation (CPR), 71-72, 79-81, 84-85, 105
  see also Artificial respiration.
Checkups
  recommended schedule, 14-15
  record of, 235
Chest pain, 73, **82**, 86, 140, 168, 174
Chicken pox, 66, **83**, 87, 173, 183, 214
Choking, 71, 72, 79, **84-85**, 92, 96, 169, 197, 205, 211
Cold, 74, 75, 82, **86**, 87, 92, 102, 106, 127, 148, 151, 156, 165, 168, 185, 195, 207
Cold sore, 66, 78, **87**, 125, 135, 204
Colic, **88**
Coma, 100
Concussion, **89**
Constipation, 54, 88, **90**, 98, 192, 205
Convulsion, 70, **91**, 110, 169, 203, 211
Cough, 56, 74, 75, 86, **92**, 96, 98, 103, 111, 144, 148, 151, 168, 177, 197, 206, 209, 216
Cradle cap, **93**
Creeping eruption, 67, **94**
Croup, 52, 56, 71-72, 75, 84-85, 86, 92, **96**, 103, 111, 148, 216

U

Umbilical cord infection, **210**
Unconsciousness, 70, 79-81, 89, 91, 104, 105, 109, 130, 132, 140-141, 142, 169, **211**
Urinary tract infection, 58, 60, 100, **212**

V

Vaccination
  see Immunization.
Virus, 92, 102, 110, 121, 125, 133, 138, 144, 151, 155, 156, 159, 171, 177, 183, 191, 195, 214, 215

Vision problem, 95, 136, 169, 196, 206, 211, **213**
  see also Eyes.
Vomiting, 52, 54, 91, 99, 102, 104, 110, 127, 130, 133, 134, 141, 144, 151, 152, 157, 159, 160, 161, 169, 171, 173, 177, 179, 191, 192, 193, 197, 201, 211, **214**, 216

W

Wart, **215**
Weight problems, 34-37
Whooping cough, 75, 92, 96, **216**

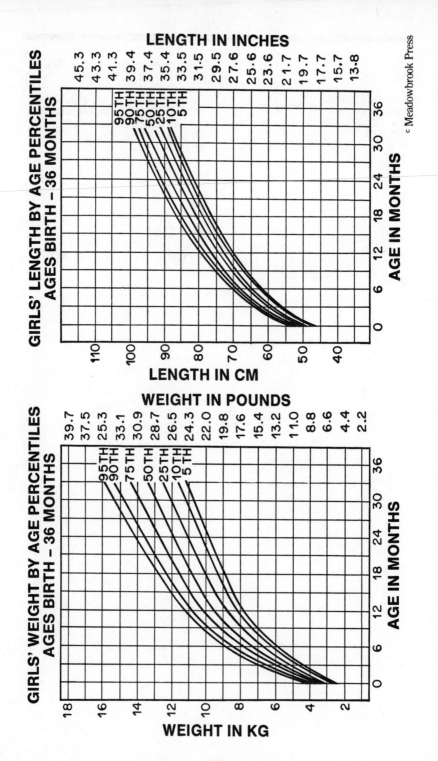

LENGTH IN INCHES

GIRLS' LENGTH BY AGE PERCENTILES
AGES BIRTH – 36 MONTHS

95TH
90TH
75TH
50TH
25TH
10TH
5TH

45.3 43.3 41.3 39.4 37.4 35.4 33.5 31.5 29.5 27.6 25.6 23.6 21.7 19.7 17.7 15.7 13.8

36 30 24 18 12 6 0

AGE IN MONTHS

110 100 90 80 70 60 50 40

LENGTH IN CM

© Meadowbrook Press

WEIGHT IN POUNDS

GIRLS' WEIGHT BY AGE PERCENTILES
AGES BIRTH – 36 MONTHS

95TH
90TH
75TH
50TH
25TH
10TH
5TH

39.7 37.5 25.3 33.1 30.9 28.7 26.5 24.3 22.0 19.8 17.6 15.4 13.2 11.0 8.8 6.6 4.4 2.2

36 30 24 18 12 6 0

AGE IN MONTHS

18 16 14 12 10 8 6 4 2

WEIGHT IN KG

230

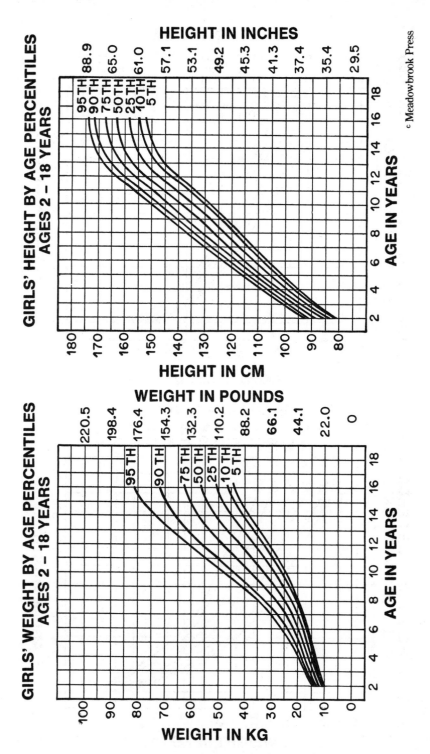

GIRLS' HEIGHT BY AGE PERCENTILES
AGES 2 – 18 YEARS

HEIGHT IN INCHES

88.9
65.0
61.0
57.1
53.1
49.2
45.3
41.3
37.4
35.4
29.5

95TH
90TH
75TH
50TH
25TH
10TH
5TH

AGE IN YEARS

180
170
160
150
140
130
120
110
100
90
80

HEIGHT IN CM

GIRLS' WEIGHT BY AGE PERCENTILES
AGES 2 – 18 YEARS

WEIGHT IN POUNDS

220.5
198.4
176.4
154.3
132.3
110.2
88.2
66.1
44.1
22.0
0

95TH
90TH
75TH
50TH
25TH
10TH
5TH

AGE IN YEARS

100
90
80
70
60
50
40
30
20
10
0

WEIGHT IN KG

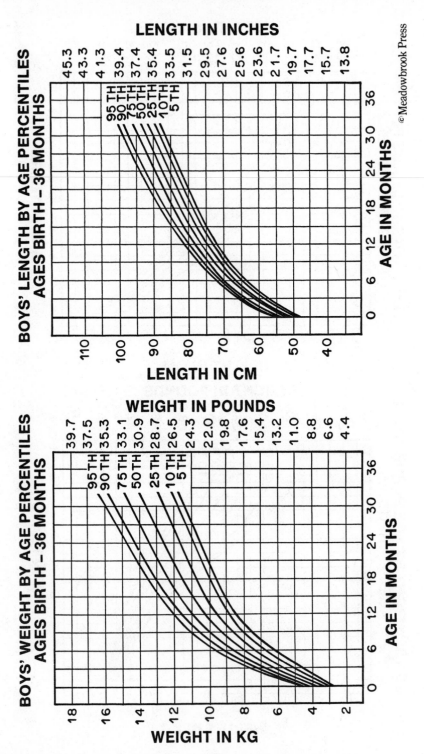

LENGTH IN INCHES

©Meadowbrook Press

BOYS' LENGTH BY AGE PERCENTILES AGES BIRTH – 36 MONTHS

45.3 43.3 41.3 39.4 37.4 35.4 33.5 31.5 29.5 27.6 25.6 23.6 21.7 19.7 17.7 15.7 13.8

95TH 90TH 75TH 50TH 25TH 10TH 5TH

AGE IN MONTHS

0 6 12 18 24 30 36

110 100 90 80 70 60 50 40

LENGTH IN CM

WEIGHT IN POUNDS

BOYS' WEIGHT BY AGE PERCENTILES AGES BIRTH – 36 MONTHS

39.7 37.5 35.3 33.1 30.9 28.7 26.5 24.3 22.0 19.8 17.6 15.4 13.2 11.0 8.8 6.6 4.4

95TH 90TH 75TH 50TH 25TH 10TH 5TH

AGE IN MONTHS

0 6 12 18 24 30 36

18 16 14 12 10 8 6 4 2

WEIGHT IN KG

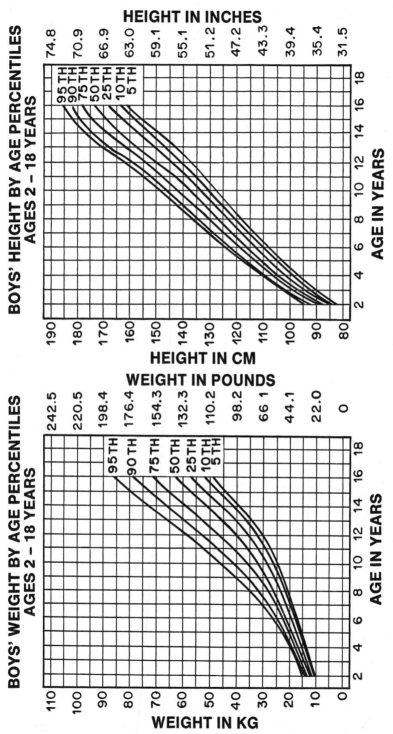

HEIGHT IN INCHES

BOYS' HEIGHT BY AGE PERCENTILES
AGES 2 – 18 YEARS

74.8
70.9
66.9
63.0
59.1
55.1
51.2
47.2
43.3
39.4
35.4
31.5

95TH
90TH
75TH
50TH
25TH
10TH
5TH

AGE IN YEARS

190
180
170
160
150
140
130
120
110
100
90
80

HEIGHT IN CM

WEIGHT IN POUNDS

BOYS' WEIGHT BY AGE PERCENTILES
AGES 2 – 18 YEARS

242.5
220.5
198.4
176.4
154.3
132.3
110.2
98.2
66 1
44.1
22.0
0

95TH
90TH
75TH
50TH
25TH
10TH
5TH

AGE IN YEARS

110
100
90
80
70
60
50
40
30
20
10
0

WEIGHT IN KG

233

IMMUNIZATION RECORD

For _____

	Recommended Age	Date Given	Dosage/ Preparation	Reaction
1. DTP (diphtheria, tetanus & pertussis)	2 months		_____	
DTP	4 months		_____	
DTP	6 months		_____	
DTP	1½ yrs.		_____	
DTP	4–6 yrs.		_____	
2. Oral Polio Vaccine	2 months		_____	
Oral Polio Vaccine	4 months		_____	
Oral Polio Vaccine	6 months (optional)		_____	
Oral Polio Vaccine	1½ yrs.		_____	
Oral Polio Vaccine	4–6 yrs.		_____	
3. Measles Virus Vaccine Live	15 months			
4. Mumps	15 months			
5. Rubella (German measles)	15 months			
6. Tetanus/Diphtheria (adult type)	14–16 yrs.		_____	
			_____	

7. Others

_____

_____

_____

_____

_____

_____

EXAMINATIONS & OFFICE CALLS

For _____

DATE	AGE	LENGTH/ HEIGHT	WEIGHT	HEAD CIRC. (Infants)	PROBLEMS, DIAGNOSES, LABORATORY AND OTHER FINDINGS	DOCTOR'S ADVICE AND COMMENTS

WHEN YOU CAN'T TAKE ASPIRIN,

HEALTH PROFESSIONALS RECOMMEND

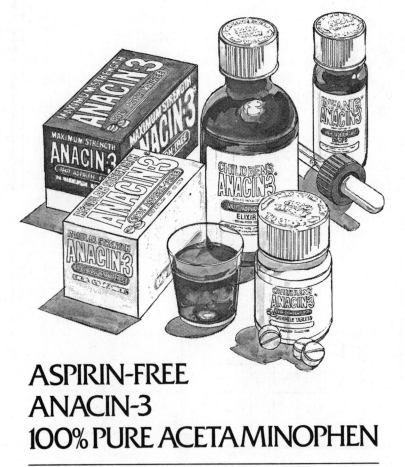

ASPIRIN-FREE
ANACIN-3
100% PURE ACETAMINOPHEN

WHITEHALL LABORATORIES
Division of American Home Products Corporation
685 THIRD AVENUE, NEW YORK, NEW YORK 10017

EXECUTIVE OFFICES   (212) 878-5500

Dear Parents:

We at Whitehall Laboratories are pleased to provide you with "The Parent's Guide to Baby and Child Medical Care." We are sure you will find it to be an informative and useful reference.

We also hope you will use the attached coupon to save on any of our Anacin-3® products. Anacin-3, 100% aspirin-free...all available in tamper-resistant packages.

Sincerely,

Edward V. Henry, M.D.
Vice President-Medical Affairs

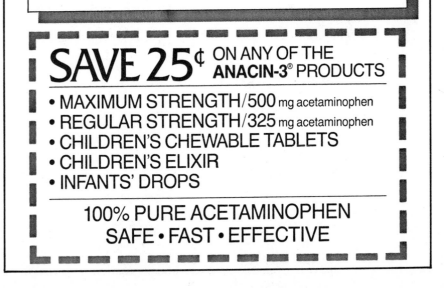